TECH-NO TO TECH PRO

A PRACTICAL GUIDE TO DIGITAL VISIBILITY WITHOUT LOSING YOUR HUMANITY

LEILA KUBESCH

LANTERN GROVE PRESS

Tech-No to Tech-Pro A Practical Guide to Digital Visibility Without Losing Your Humanity

Published by Lantern Grove Press

First Edition 2025
Printed in the United States of America

PREFACE

Why Visibility Matters Now

This book is for those who want to make a difference and know that being seen is part of that work. Whether you're an educator, entrepreneur, coach, or business owner, you already lead with purpose.

The challenge isn't effort. It's visibility, it's how to be seen in a world that moves faster than any classroom, boardroom, or client call.

When I first joined onto LinkedIn, I didn't see anyone who looked or sounded like me. I wasn't sure what to post or how to sound "professional." It took time and a lot of small, awkward experiments to realize that visibility isn't performance. It's presence.

This book is the guide I wish I had at the start, using plain language, real examples, and lessons learned through trial, error, and persistence. You'll find practical tools grounded in lived experience so you can show up online without losing your humanity.

Each chapter begins with a story followed by the insight behind it, then closes with a short summary with tips and reflection prompts. The book unfolds in three parts: Communicate, Connect, and Collaborate, the 3 Cs that guide everything I teach. By the end you will know how to use digital tools to express your message clearly, build meaningful relationships, and create impact that lasts.

Read it like a conversation. Pause where it speaks to you. Try what feels possible.

And when you start to see the difference visibility makes, not in likes or followers, but in doors that open and voices that rise beside yours, pass it on.

Facts inform. Emotion connects. Your website can explain what you do, but it's your visibility that shows why it matters. That is what draws people to you and keeps them coming back.

ACKNOWLEDGEMENTS

To everyone who believed that visibility is belonging, thank you for seeing before others could. Your encouragement, laughter, and stories shaped this book. To the educators, coaches, and dreamers who keep asking questions and showing up, you are the reason this work exists.

About the Author

Leila Kubesch is an international keynote speaker, educator, and storyteller who empowers others to use their voice and visibility for impact. She is a National Teachers Hall of Fame inductee, and founder of Parents2Partners.org. Through her photography, talks, and workshops, she inspires communities to communicate, connect, and collaborate for lasting change.

QUICK START: HOW TO GET THE MOST FROM THIS BOOK

You don't need to read this book in order.

Each chapter stands on its own as a story, a lesson, and a small step forward. Start with what pulls your attention. If you're new to digital visibility, begin with the early chapters. If you're ready to deepen connection, skip ahead to collaboration or reflection.

Bring a notebook or a few sticky notes. Pause when a story reminds you of your own. Jot down what you could try, not what you should do, but what feels possible.

At the end, you'll find tools and worksheets to help you put everything into practice.

Let's find out

READING MAP

How to Navigate This Book

This book unfolds in three parts, each guided by one of the 3 Cs: Communicate, Connect, and Collaborate. Think of them as the rhythm of visibility: how you show up, how you build trust, and how you sustain impact.

Part I — Communicate: The Courage to Be Seen

Focus: Communication

How to use your voice with clarity and authenticity. These chapters invite you to show up with purpose, share your story without performance, and reclaim visibility as an act of service rather than self-promotion.

Chapters 1–4:

1. When a Deer Halted My Flight (and My Excuses)

2. Being Seen Without Losing Yourself

3. The Year I Had One Follower

4. What Does Brand Mean in a Profile?

Part II — Connect: Turn Intention into Momentum

Focus: Connection

How to transform visibility into meaningful relationships. Here you'll learn how to engage, post, and comment with sincerity. Each story shows how connection grows through reciprocity, curiosity, and generosity.

Chapters 5–11:

Part III — Collaborate: Turn Visibility into Legacy

Focus: Collaboration

How to turn engagement into partnership and presence into legacy. This final section helps you sustain your visibility while protecting your energy. You'll discover how clarity, collaboration, and follow-through keep your work alive long after a post or presentation ends.

Chapters 12–23:

21. Tools That Multiply Your Time

22. Do You Need LinkedIn Premium to Grow?

How to Use This Book

Each chapter follows a simple rhythm:

- First the story, a real moment that sparked a shift
- The lesson learned from what it revealed
- Tips & tools for practical steps you can apply right away
- Reflection prompts to turn new insight into meaningful action

You can read straight through or open to the section you need most today. By the time you finish, you'll have your own roadmap for communicating clearly, connecting with purpose, and collaborating with impact.

TABLE OF CONTENTS

1

WHEN A DEER HALTED MY FLIGHT (AND MY EXCUSES)

Sometimes clarity doesn't arrive through reflection or planning. Sometimes it lands with a jolt, a sound, a laugh, a pause that stops everything you thought you were sure of.

It began for me during a small late afternoon regional flight. I settled into my seat hoping to avoid small talk and enjoyed a quiet flight. After descending and on our way to the gate, the pilot's voice came over the intercom, "Folks, we've just hit a deer. Sit back, hang tight. We'll be here for a while before we head to the gate." Then he started singing, "A deer in the gear!"

The man beside me leaned over and whispered "the pilot's weird." We both burst out laughing, and that laugh turned into an hour-long conversation.

As we reached the gate and were about to deplane, he took out his phone and asked if I was on LinkedIn? I asked "on what?" He repeated himself, smiled, and tore a napkin from the tray table. He wrote LinkedIn on it, handed it to me along with a $25 Amazon gift card, and said, "Buy the book Traction. You'll thank me later."

When I got home, I stared at that napkin for days before creating my first profile. It felt awkward. I didn't know what to say in my profile or how to say it. He became my first follower and was the only one for an entire year.

Embarrassed I tried to delete my account but couldn't figure out how. I spent an entire afternoon clicking through settings, growing more frustrated by the minute. I felt trapped between wanting to disappear and not knowing how. I finally decided that I could either learn how to delete it or learn how to use it, and I chose the latter.

Today I have more than 20,000 followers, but numbers alone don't define success. Visibility isn't about popularity, it's about purpose and learning to leverage relationships you create, sharing meaning, and bringing value to others. I still think back to that flight and laugh at the pilot's voice echoing through the cabin "a deer in the gear!" A single, ridiculous moment changed how I saw connection forever.

I also think of a scene from Rush Hour of Jackie Chan jumping out of a car singing *"Huh! Yeah! What is it good for?"* The query applies here too. The question isn't what social media is good for, but how it could be good for us if we leverage it well.

You don't need a marketing degree to build trust or tech expertise to grow. Presence begins the moment you decide to try.

I wasn't afraid of hard work or learning, I was afraid of being seen. I wanted to look my best and not be caught off guard or seen as imperfect. Most days, however, aren't picture-perfect. Sometimes I'm in mismatched pajamas and eating cereal for dinner. I grew up believing that visibility was risky, determined not to stand out or draw attention, so I worked quietly. I wasn't chasing attention; I was avoiding it. But when you stay quiet long enough, people start to believe you have nothing to say. I had plenty to say, I just didn't know where to start. Have you ever felt like that? Eventually I realized the question isn't "what is it good for?" but "what could it be good for if used with purpose?"

For me, social media isn't about being seen. It's about being of use. Visibility doesn't begin with an audience; it begins with a choice. The choice to raise your head, speak your truth, and share what you've built even if your hands shake. The goal isn't to be famous, it's to be findable by the right people. The goal isn't to be followed, it's to be felt when they think your content resonates with them.

When you use your voice with purpose, visibility stops being about you and becomes a gift to everyone who needs your story to begin their own.

Chapter Summary

- Connection often begins in unexpected moments.
- Visibility grows from curiosity and courage, not strategy.
- Purpose gives visibility power; numbers don't.
- The goal isn't perfection, it is presence.

Tips

- Keep a small "visibility journal" of people or opportunities that appear because you shared something.
- When hesitation creeps in, remember the napkin. Small gestures open big doors.
- Revisit early posts to see your progress, it's proof that you've grown.

Reflection & Application

1. When did you last say yes to something that scared you but changed you?
2. Who offered you a small push that set bigger things in motion?
3. How could you use one piece of your story?

Bridge to Chapter 2

Sometimes staying quiet doesn't just shrink your world, it can silently erase the good work all around you. That feeling of pride disappearing and being unseen is something I know well. In the next chapter, I'll share how silence can erase the stories of those we lead and how stepping into visibility on their behalf changed everything for me.

2

BEING SEEN WITHOUT LOSING YOURSELF

My students arrived early. Girls were getting their hair braided, boys were borrowing ties and rehearsing interview questions. They were excited because a newspaper reporter was meeting them after school. However, when the journalist never showed I learned how silence could erase good work.

When the last bell rang, they packed in silence, hope shrinking into confusion. I wanted to say something to make it better but the words stuck in my throat. Instead, I smiled and told them we'd take a group picture anyway, my small attempt to capture their pride even if nobody else would see it. That snapshot became the start of our own archive and proof that their work mattered no matter who was watching. That was the moment I learned that when we stay invisible, even good work can disappear.

For years I believed that good work spoke for itself. I focused on results, pulling late nights, making quiet fixes, and having the satisfaction of seeing things improve. Recognition wasn't the point. I thought staying humble meant staying silent.

Then one afternoon, that belief unraveled.

During a school event, our principal thanked a teacher and her students for raising funds and starting a much-needed recycling program. The teacher smiled. My eighth graders looked horrified. "But we're the ones who did it, Ms. K!" they whispered. They were right. They had planned the campaign, created the posters, and organized the pickup. I had guided them through it all remaining in the background, assuming the results of the work would tell its own story. It didn't.

In that moment, I realized that my silence didn't just hide me, it erased them. Being invisible wasn't protecting my humility, it was denying my students the visibility they deserved.

I had even invited the local paper to feature their project, but no one showed up. The kids waited, dressed in their best, beaming with pride that never got shared. Watching their disappointment that day was the moment I understood how much it matters to be seen.

After that day I began documenting everything. I took photos of their work, their teamwork, and their small wins. This was long before social media, just snapshots on a disposable camera and notes in a folder. Without realizing it, I had begun a mission that would shape everything I do through giving voice and visibility to others.

That experience stayed with me. Years later when I finally created a LinkedIn profile, that same instinct resurfaced. I wasn't posting to show off, I was documenting progress, amplifying effort, and making sure stories of impact didn't get lost again.

Visibility, I learned, isn't self-promotion; it's storytelling. It's making sure that people, ideas, and lessons don't disappear because no one took the time to share them.

Learning to Step Forward Without Stepping Over

1.Document the journey, not just the outcome: Snapshots, notes, and short reflections preserve stories others might miss.

2. Share credit often: Visibility is about shining a light, not owning it. Name your collaborators. Honor your team.

3. Use visibility as advocacy: When you highlight someone's work, you give them dignity and a sense of belonging.

4. Stay rooted in truth: Don't wait for perfection. Share moments as they happen, they're more powerful that way.

5. Connect purpose to every post: Ask who might this story encourage or empower? Let your answer guide what you share.

Chapter Summary

- Staying invisible may feel safe but can erase meaningful work.
- Visibility honors effort and gives others a platform to be seen.
- Documenting and sharing builds advocacy, not ego.
- Purposeful visibility amplifies collective impact.

Tips

- Keep a simple photo log of moments worth remembering, faces, projects, and teamwork.
- When you post online, tag or mention those who helped; it builds trust and community.
- If an effort gets overlooked, tell the story anyway. Someone needs to hear it.

Reflection & Application

1. When has your silence unintentionally hidden someone else's contribution?
2. What story from your work deserves to be shared but hasn't been told yet?
3. How might visibility become a form of advocacy in your role?
4. What small action could you take this week to make someone else's impact visible?

Bridge to Chapter 3

It took years, and a lot of snapshots and stories, to understand that sharing doesn't diminish humility but instead it multiplies impact. Even after that lesson, showing up online wasn't easy. Next, I'll take you back to the year I had just one follower and how that awkward beginning turned into a foundation for real, lasting visibility. With those stories in mind, let's turn to how the smallest act of showing up can transform the outcome for people and projects you care about

3

THE YEAR I HAD ONE FOLLOWER

I sat cross-legged on the floor, laptop open, scrolling through perfect profiles. Everyone else seemed smarter, smoother, more professional. I revised, deleted, and started again, wishing someone would just show me how.

When I first created my LinkedIn profile, I had no idea what I was doing. I copied ideas from someone else, like a student sneaking a peek at a neighbor's test to discover their answers were wrong too. That's when I wished I had a real guide.

In this chapter, you'll learn how to create a strong foundation for your profile, the part of digital visibility that speaks for you when you're not in the room.

First Step: Build a Complete Profile

The first time I saw my own profile thumbnail next to a post, I winced. The photo was years old, the banner blank, and my headline vague. That moment taught me that when online, people meet our details before they meet us.

A completed profile earns *30 percent more weekly views*. Think of it as your digital handshake, every section builds credibility. You wouldn't offer a few fingers, you use the entire hand.

1. Profile Photo

- Use a clear, recent headshot with good lighting and a simple background.
- Photos with real people, especially you, get 60 percent more reach.
- Avoid stock or heavily filtered images. They underperform by nearly half.

2. Banner Image

- Your banner should represent what you do or stand for.
- Use it for visual storytelling by showing your field, your work in action, or your mission.
- Use the full space to showcase a 3D model of your book, your design, or another creative element. Include yourself in action, not just on stage, and add a brief overview of what you do and the impact you aim to create.

3. Headline

This is the most-searched field after your name.

Instead of a job title, write a short value statement like:

HR Leader : Building workplaces where people grow, belong, and lead with heart.

Clothes Designer: Designing garments that move with life, made to be lived in, not just worn.

Photographer: Capturing connection in every frame where moments turn into meaning.

Use simple language so it sounds friendly and easy to understand. Also aim for clarity, not cleverness.

4. About Section

This is your *"why."* Keep it conversational and mission-focused.

Structure:

- **Line 1:** What you do and why it matters.
- **Line 2:** Who you help.
- **Line 3:** How people can reach or work with you.

Avoid jargon and write in the first person. Readers should feel like they are meeting you.

5. Experience

- List what you accomplished not just where you worked.
- Use verbs that show impact like 'led', 'created', 'developed', 'partnered'.
- Remember that visibility grows from results, not just responsibilities.

6. Skills and Endorsements

LinkedIn favors profiles with endorsed skills.

Choose five to ten skills related to your professional path and update them each quarter.

Ask to be endorsed for the skills you list.

7. Creator Mode (Optional): Helpful, but Not a Must

You've probably heard that to grow your reach on LinkedIn, you "must" turn on Creator Mode. But here's the truth: you don't need it to be visible.

So let's talk about what it actually does and how to decide if it's right for you.

What Creator Mode *Can* Do

- Changes your profile's main button from "Connect" to "Follow"
- Lets you highlight up to five hashtags, your topics of focus
- Prioritizes your content over your resume on your profile
- May unlock tools like LinkedIn Live, Audio Events, and analytics if you're eligible.
- I already had access to some of those features without it. So don't assume turning it on is the only path to visibility.

What Creator Mode Doesn't Do

- It doesn't make you magically go viral.
- It doesn't gatekeep features like newsletters for everyone. (Now all of us have access without it.)
- Should You Use It?

If you're:

- Actively posting
- Wanting to grow an audience
- Leading with ideas and conversation

Then yes, try it.

But if you're:

- Building quietly
- Focused on connections over followers
- Still experimenting with your content rhythm
- Then wait. You can do just fine without it.

I didn't wait for a setting to give me permission. I started with what I had and kept showing up. You can too.

Second Step: Engage with Purpose

Once your profile is complete, engagement becomes the engine for visibility. Commenting ten times a day for a month can lead to:

- 40 percent more profile views
- 25 percent higher engagement
- 20 percent more followers

I comment on ten posts in one sitting.

How to Comment Well

- Add insight, not just flattery. Go beyond "great post!" and say something real.
- Write two to three lines that expand the conversation.
- Be early! Comment in the first hour after a post goes up.
- Don't only comment to impress people with big followings. Lift up your peers, the ones doing meaningful work at your level. Your network grows sideways, not just upward.
- Use complete sentences when commenting to boost a post. Avoid short, generic phrases like "Great post,"

which make it seem like you didn't take the time to read the content.

Tagging Wisely

When you tag people directly in your post, LinkedIn assumes they are part of the conversation. If they do not respond quickly, usually within the first hour, your post can lose momentum. The algorithm reads silence as less engagement. Other data showed that it needs to be within the first 30 minutes.

A simple workaround is to mention people instead of tagging them. For example, write their name naturally in your post or comment, such as "I learned this from Maria Lopez," rather than using the "@" tag.

If you want to tag, use the comments section instead of the main post. It looks cleaner and does not risk slowing your reach if the person does not reply

Photos and Posts

Avoid using ChatGPT to edit your work. According to marketers at the GHL conference, content created this way rarely performs well because it often loses its heart and soul. I tested it myself. The writing was fast and polished, but it changed my tone completely and sounded like AI wrote it.

You can usually tell when content is AI generated. For example: "This workshop is not just a workshop, it is commitment, community, and connection."

Nobody actually talks like that. My workshop is exactly that, a hands-on training program.

We don't need to illustrate keywords like "networking" with a fake bird's-eye view of a cluster of people. We already know what networking looks like.

- Posts with real people outperform stock photos by 45%.
- A photo of you can raise reach by 60%.
- Optimal post length is 900–1,200 characters.

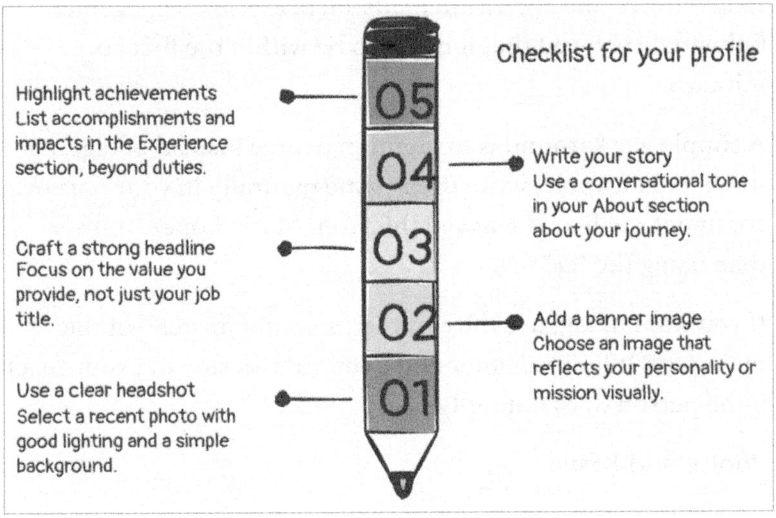

Third Step: Post Like a Pro

Your content is how people experience you before they meet you.

What to Post

- 40 percent: Solving problems (practical advice)
- 40 percent: Sharing perspectives (thought leadership)
- 20 percent: Telling stories (emotional connection)

Posting Frequency

LinkedIn boosts one post at a time. Wait at least four hours before posting again, otherwise your earlier post will get ignored by the algorithm.

Avoid These Pitfalls

- Posts asking for "likes" or "shares." You'll lose 50 percent of your reach.
- Including external links drops reach by 40–50 percent.
- Using overly ornate formatting including excessive line breaks making your content hard to read.
- Do not post and disappear ("post and ghost"). If you don't reply to comments, your reach takes a 25–40 percent hit.

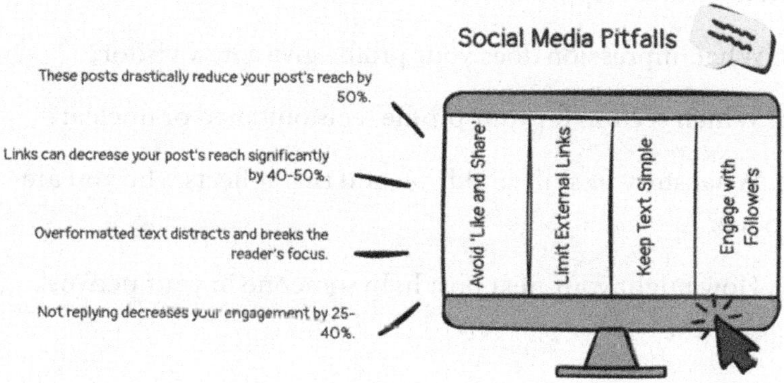

Chapter Summary

- A complete profile builds more trust and generates more interest to connect with you.
- Signing up for Creator Mode and engaging with consistent commenting expands visibility.
- Using real human photos and concise writing drive engagement.

- Clarity, connection, and consistency always outperform gimmicks.

Tips

- Review your profile on a mobile device; 65 percent of users are on their phones.
- Add a banner that aligns with your message.
- Collect posts that inspire you and keep an inspiration file.
- Refresh your headline and 'about' section every ninety days.

Reflection & Application

1. What impression does your profile give a new visitor?

2. Which section on your profile feels outdated or unclear?

3. What story or skill could you add that reflects who you are today?

4. How might your next post help someone in your network right now?

Bridge to Chapter 4

Crafting your digital presence isn't just about getting noticed, it's about making it easier for others to connect with you for the right reasons. Next, let's dive into how your brand is not a logo or a fancy tagline, but the everyday promise you make whenever you show up, both online and off.

4

WHAT DOES BRAND MEAN IN A PROFILE?

For the longest time, I didn't know what people meant by *brand.* When I first heard, "You've got to build your personal brand," I thought *I'm not a company. I'm just me.*

When you work in education or run a small business, "brand" can sound pretentious, like something reserved for people with billboards or teams in matching shirts.

But I later learned that your brand is simply the promise you make when you show up. It's how people recognize you. Not by your hairstyle or logo, but by your tone, your consistency, and your presence. A friend in the engineering industry put it well: "*I want people, when they talk about engineering, to think of me as the go-to guy.*"

The Hair-Down Lesson

Recently I hired a photographer for new headshots. Friends urged me to wear my hair down. "You'll look softer" they said. So I did, for all the photos.

The shots were stunning. Perfect lighting, beautiful composition. And a complete waste of money.

Because I never wear my hair down. Not on stage. Not at home. Not ever. When I looked at those photos, I didn't see myself, I saw someone pretending to be me.

That was the day I understood branding. A brand isn't what looks best on camera, it's what still feels right in real life. I no longer take advice because it often feels like "add vice." What we really need are options, ideas, and inspiration that make an impact, not pressure to follow one path. What works for someone else may not work for everyone.

A Brand Is Alignment, Not Aesthetic

Your brand isn't about fonts or colors, it's about familiarity. When someone meets you online, they should feel like they've already met you in person. Be consistent in how you show up, what you share, and the values you express. That's how you create a brand that speaks to the people you want to attract.

That means:

- If your emails are warm but your posts sound robotic, something's off.
- If your photo looks like it belongs to a stranger, change it.
- If your humor usually lands better in person than in writing, try writing in a conversational tone.

A consistent brand doesn't mean being polished, it means being *predictable in the best way*. When people know what to expect from you, they come back.

How to Build a Brand That Feels Like You

- Keep your tone steady. If you are kind in person, let that kindness carry into your words.

- Update your photo regularly. People remember faces long before they remember résumés.
- Use your own words. If you would not say it out loud, it does not belong in a post.
- Revisit your profile often. As you grow and your message shifts, let your profile grow with you.
- Stay visible but stay real. You do not need to be loud to be seen.

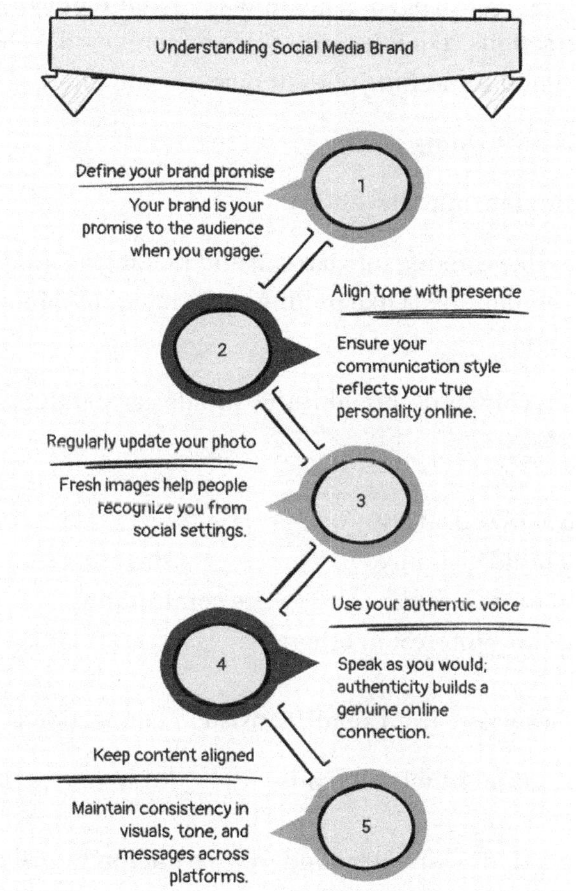

Testing Your Voice by Commenting Before You Post

Before I ever posted on LinkedIn, I lurked. I scrolled through other people's posts, quietly observing.

What did other users say? How did they sound so natural? How did they get hundreds of comments while I could barely think of one sentence to write?

I told myself I was *researching,* but really, I was hiding.

Then I noticed something small but powerful: people who commented before posting got noticed. Their names appeared in conversations. Their insights were remembered. When they finally shared something of their own, people cared.

That was my turning point.

Why Commenting Matters

Posting is like walking into a room and making an announcement. Commenting is like pulling up a chair and joining the conversation.

When you comment thoughtfully, you do several things at once:

- You show curiosity.
- You build visibility.
- You practice finding your voice comfortably.
- You show interest in others.

Confidence grows from small, consistent connections.

How to Comment with Purpose

- Read, don't skim. Respond to what's actually written and not what you assume.
- Add, don't echo. Instead of saying "great post," offer a brief insight or example.

- Be genuine. If you disagree, do it kindly. Respect keeps doors open.
- Tag thoughtfully. Mention someone only if your comment truly relates to them.
- Keep it human. Write as if you're speaking across a table, not typing into a void.
- Offer a different perspective. I once read a post where someone said that elderly people are not respected. I replied that I had not noticed this sentiment because, in other countries, I saw the opposite, older adults are treated as wise and valued for the wisdom they share.

Thoughtful comments quietly build reputation. It's digital word-of-mouth, subtle but powerful.

Practical Prompts

- Spend ten minutes a day commenting *before* you post.
- Lift up voices with low engagement in your field.
- Ask a question instead of dropping an opinion.

End your comment with a question that invites a response. For example, you could say, "I would love to know what tips you have about this," or "How have you seen this work in your field?" or "That made me think, does that match your experience?" This keeps the conversation going and helps build meaningful connections.

Chapter Summary

- our brand isn't decoration. It's the feeling people get when they find you online.
- Authenticity outperforms polish.
- Consistency builds recognition and trust.

- Commenting helps you practice visibility and gain confidence.

Tips

- Review your online presence every quarter. Small tweaks keep your profile aligned with your brand.
- Ask a trusted friend what three words describe you online and compare them with how you want to be seen.
- Keep your visuals, tone, and message aligned across platforms.
- Comment thoughtfully before posting. It strengthens your brand and help to build genuine connections.

Reflection & Application

1. When have you presented a version of yourself that didn't feel authentic?

2. If someone only saw your comments, what would they learn about you?

3. How can you make your digital presence feel more like you in real life?

4. What's one small way you can engage today that reflects your true voice?

Bridge to Chapter 5

As we unearth why visibility matters, the next chapter provides practical tools for commenting and growing your digital presence thoughtfully.

5

THE BLOT METHOD

I used to stare at a blinking cursor like it was a dare. What do you say online when you're not sure if anyone's listening. Or worse, when you're afraid they are? I remember sitting cross-legged on the floor, laptop open, scrolling through perfect posts. Everyone else seemed to have a plan.

Then I realized that writing online isn't about sounding right; it's about being *real*.

Why Connection Matters

When I finally started posting, it was clear to me most people read like they scroll. Fast. If your first line doesn't catch them, the rest doesn't matter. People don't read to find you, they read to find *themselves* in what you say. Visibility online isn't about being impressive. It's about being relatable, and relatability starts with a *story*.

What is the Storytelling BLOT Method?

The BLOT Method has two versions. One helps you write clearly and concisely. The other helps you write stories that connect. I use both depending on the goal.

1. BLOT for Clarity: Bottom Line On Top

This version is often used in business or government writing. The idea is simple: start with your main point, then explain. People are busy, and this gets straight to what matters.

Example

Bottom Line On Top We completed the first phase of the project two weeks ahead of schedule.

Link for Context Our team worked with partners in three cities and streamlined the review process.

Outcome / Result This saved us both time and cost, allowing us to move to phase two sooner than expected.

Tie-back / Next Step We'll continue using this workflow to keep our momentum going.

Why it works: It's clear, quick, and easy to understand. Perfect for reports, proposals, or business updates.

2. BLOT for Storytelling: Beginning, Lesson, Outcome, Takeaway.

This is the version I use most. It's personal, emotional, and human. I've used it to write grant proposals that won funding, articles that got published, LinkedIn posts that reached thousands, and now, scripts that hold attention from the very first line.

Example

Beginning A student once told me, "I can't write stories because nothing interesting ever happens to me."

Lesson I learned that everyone has stories; they just need someone to help them see the value in their everyday moments.

Outcome We started writing short daily reflections, and within weeks, even the quietest students were sharing pieces that made the class laugh and cry.

Takeaway We all have a story worth sharing. The real question is, who are you giving permission to tell theirs?

Why it works: It makes your message stick. It helps your reader or listener feel something, not just understand something.

The Storytelling BLOT: A Poetic Reminder

(Beginning, Lesson, Outcome, Takeaway — the rhythm of connection)

When you post online, don't rush to the end,
Begin with a story, a spark to send.
A moment you lived, a truth you've found —
That's where real connection's bound.

Then share the lesson, small or grand,
The thing you learned that shaped your stand.
It's not the title, stage, or view —
It's what that moment taught to you.

Next comes the outcome — what changed inside,
What shifted, grew, or multiplied.
It's how your insight took its flight,
Turning a scroll into shared light.

And end with a takeaway, honest and clear —
A line they'll remember, a reason to hear.
Ask them a question, spark their say —
That's storytelling BLOT, the human way.

So when you post, don't sell or shout,
Just start with heart — and let it out.
Because visibility isn't a game to play,
It's how we remind the world — we've got something to say.

— Leila Kubesch

Use the first BLOT: Bottom Line On Top when you need to **get things done.** Use the second, BLOT for Storytelling: Beginning, Lesson, Outcome, Takeaway when you want to **move hearts and inspire action.**

How to Write Posts That Connect

1. **Start strong.** Begin with a moment, question, or emotion, not a summary.

2. **Keep it short.** Posts between 900 -1,200 characters perform best.

3. **Break lines for breath.** Space creates rhythm; rhythm keeps readers scrolling.

4. **Stay conversational.** Write like you're speaking to one person who needs it.

5. **Show, don't preach.** Share the moment that taught the lesson.

6. **Use photos with people.** Posts featuring real faces get 45–60% more reach.

7. **Engage back.** Reply to comments. Visibility grows through conversation, not broadcast.

What to Post

When people struggle to post online, it's rarely because they lack ideas. It's because they overthink what belongs on their page. This simple guide breaks down four types of posts that keep your content balanced, consistent, and engaging. Think of it as your compass for showing up online with purpose.

1. Educate

These posts share knowledge, simplify a process, or solve a problem. They position you as a trusted guide in your field. Examples include "how-to" tips, short infographics, or myth-busting facts that correct common misconceptions. Even a simple Q&A format can draw engagement because people love learning something useful.

Goal: Teach something in a way that makes life easier for your audience.

2. Elevate

These posts inspire. They lift your audience and show the heart behind your brand. You might share a personal story, a favorite quote, a daily affirmation, or a "before and after" example that reminds people growth is possible.

Goal: Create connection through encouragement.

3. Entertain

People come to social media to connect and to feel something. Use humor, trends, or storytelling to keep your content relatable and human. A lighthearted meme, a story that makes people nod and say "me too," or a clever trend adapted to your niche can make your message stick.

Goal: Build familiarity and fun while keeping your personality front and center.

4. Sell

This is where you invite your audience to take action. Share testimonials, success stories, or case studies that show real results. Explain what you offer and how it helps. Selling doesn't have to feel pushy when it's grounded in service and stories.

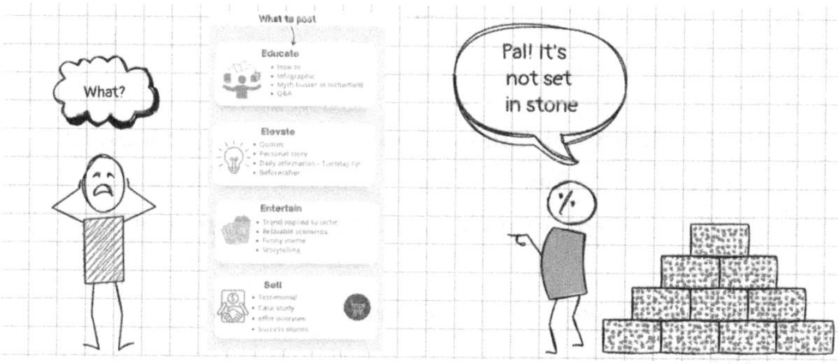

Goal: Show the value of your work through results, not just words.

If every post fits into one of these four types, Educate, Elevate, Entertain, or Sell, you'll always know what to share next. Focus on consistency. Show up online with the same energy you bring in person, and people will recognize you.

If you only post twice a week, choose Tuesday and Thursday since those are the best days to build consistency and reach. Treat it as a learning journey. Mistakes and low engagement are part of growth.

Chapter Summary

BLOT storytelling: Beginning, Lesson, Outcome, Takeaway.

- Sharing stories builds connection faster than strategy.
- Short posts, real moments, and a clear "why" make people stop scrolling.
- Engagement happens through conversation, not perfection.
- Authentic posts attract continued engagement beyond after the first hour.

Tips

- Read your post aloud. If it sounds stiff, rewrite it more like a conversation.
- Use three hashtags max. Keep them relevant, not trendy.
- Save your best-performing posts and study what worked.
- Revisit old posts quarterly. Your growth will surprise you!

Use the first BLOT when you need to **explain.**

Use the second when you want to **connect.**

Keep this page handy. Each time you write, fill in one column. With practice, you'll find that it becomes natural and easy to do.

Reflection & Application

1. What truth could you express in twelve words or less?
2. How can you make your next post easier to read at a glance?
3. Which story in your life demonstrates your core belief or lesson?
4. Who might need your message more than your perfection?

Exercise:

Write a post about your experience with learning or change using the *Storytelling BLOT Method.*

Beginning: Start with the scene or feeling.

Lesson: What did you learn?

Outcome: What happened next?

Takeaway: What can others apply?

Bridge to Chapter 6:

Before I could teach others about asking and connecting, I had to learn what happens when generosity goes unchecked. My lesson came disguised as a lunch meeting that cost me more than gas money. It taught me that boundaries aren't barriers; they protect what matters most.

6

BUILDING RELATIONSHIPS THAT LAST

How One Uncomfortable Lesson Became My Blueprint for Connection.

The drive took an hour. By the time I reached the Panera meeting place, the man who'd invited me was already eating, his papers spread across the table and his coffee half gone. Ninety minutes later, I drove home hungry, wiser, and a little embarrassed. That lunch taught me more about boundaries than any workshop ever could.

When Generosity Becomes Exhaustion

The first time I understood the importance of boundaries and reciprocity, it wasn't during a workshop or a conference, it was at a networking event.

It was new territory for me. Teachers don't often network. In schools, parents come to us, not the other way around. That evening, I hovered near the food table pretending to be busy with a plate I didn't need, wondering how everyone else seemed to know each other.

Eventually I gathered the courage to introduce myself to somebody who seemed friendly. He asked thoughtful questions and called me "a gold mine." His enthusiasm was flattering. When he suggested meeting to discuss ideas, I said yes immediately.

He chose the time and the place, a Panera about an hour from my home. The drive was long and traffic unforgiving, but I arrived on time and hungry. Inside, the line stretched out the door. I waited a few minutes until I spotted him. He was already seated, lunch in front of him, papers spread across the table. He waved me over.

From the moment I sat down, he began talking. He handed me stacks of documents including grant proposals, budgets, and program plans, and asked for my input. I answered every question, one after another. Ninety minutes passed and my stomach growled, but the conversation never paused. He ate while I worked. When I finally finished, he stood up and walked me to the door.

Once outside, he said how excited he was about all the information and how it would save him weeks of work. I asked where he had driven from, and he pointed across the street.

I drove home hungry, disappointed, and embarrassed by how much time and energy I'd given without being offered so much as a cup of tea. He'd called me invaluable yet never said thank you. The whole exchange left me uneasy.

On that drive back, I thought about what could have made it different, not just for me, but for him, too. What would a respectful, mutual, and uplifting interaction have looked like? That's when I decided that anytime someone was giving me their time or expertise, I would make it easy for them with a shorter drive, clear expectations, and tangible gratitude.

That experience taught me three powerful lessons: how to safeguard my boundaries, how to reciprocate with intention, and how to build relationships that feel steady even when the effort isn't equal. It wasn't pleasant, but it was a turning point. Before that day, I believed generosity meant saying yes to everything. Now I understand that giving is meaningful only when it's mutual, not measured.

Strong relationships are reciprocal. They're alive and they shift and stretch over time. Sometimes you give more while other times you're the one receiving support. What matters isn't keeping score but about keeping respect. In place of grand gestures, the key is awareness. When someone invests time, energy, or knowledge, they're giving part of their life. The least we can do is honor it.

I had been oblivious, assuming generosity meant saying yes to everything. Now, I understand that giving is meaningful only when it's mutual.

What the Experience Taught Me

- Reciprocity is the quiet backbone of trust. When someone helps you, people remember how seen and valued they felt.
- Boundaries protect relationships. They keep you from running on empty and make space for respect to grow.
- Respect shows up in effort. Being prepared, following through, and choosing what eases someone's load says more than words ever could.

Every meaningful partnership I've built since that day has followed the same principles: make it easy, make it personal, and make it mutual. My key word is reciprocity.

Tips for Building Relationships That Last

If you agreed too quickly and later discovered the engagement isn't a good fit, perhaps the expectations were different, then follow up right away and let them know it won't work. Never complain and never explain. Someone from the National Speakers Association once said he never works with people he doesn't like. I found that funny at first because I used to believe we didn't have that choice. I worked with people I didn't like, and my intuition proved right. They never paid me. Don't aim to please everyone. Protect your time, energy, and integrity. Here are a few reminders:

- Make giving easy. When you ask for someone's time, meet them where they are, in spirit or in person. Keep the logistics simple.
- Follow up with gratitude. A handwritten note, a photo, or a brief thank you goes a long way. It does not need to be big, only sincere.
- Offer reciprocity, not repayment. Ask how you can support what they are working on instead of focusing on paying them back.
- Set boundaries. Know your limits with time, energy, and emotional bandwidth. Boundaries are quiet agreements you keep with yourself.
- Reflect before you say yes. Ask whether it feels right and whether both of you will walk away better for it.

Chapter Summary

- The best relationships aren't balanced by numbers, they are balanced by respect.
- Visibility keeps good work alive and boundaries keep good energy intact.
- Reciprocity turns giving into growth.
- Boundaries make space for authenticity.

- Relationships that last are built on awareness, not obligation.

Reflection & Application

1. Recall a time when you overextended yourself. What boundary could have made that experience healthier?

2. Who in your circle has modeled generosity with grace? What can you learn from them?

3. How can you make it easier for others to say yes when you ask for help?

4. What small ritual could you adopt to express gratitude consistently?

5. Which connections are healthy and which others might need space, so you are giving by choice a not a feeling of obligation?

Bridge to Chapter 7

Boundaries make our relationships real and clarity helps them last. What we believe and say out loud or online shapes our connections and our future. Are you ready to make language your ally? The next three tenets will help turn intention into impact, one word, one ask, and one shift at a time.

7

THE POWER OF MINDSET AND HOW LANGUAGE SHAPES OUTCOMES

On my twentieth year of teaching, I emptied everything I had in my classroom into the trash can (gently, in case anyone wanted them). That single act, equal parts grief and relief, became the first spark of the three tenets that would shape my life.

Before I begin, I will share with you the three tenets I go by when it comes to social media and visibility:

1. You can do everything you want, just not at the same time.

2. Speak for the opportunities you desire.

3. Know that your words create your world.

Tenet One: You Can Do Everything, Just Not at the Same Time

I'll briefly explain why I believe this.

After I took everything I had from my classroom and put it in the trash can, I went straight to HR, and resigned. When I went home and told my husband, he said, "I was wondering when that would happen," because I'm married to a saint.

Before that day, I was teaching at a high school. With the largely disadvantaged group of students I worked with, I frequently saw hard things. Some would cry and tell me they were aging out of foster care. After that I often wouldn't see them again. Later, I heard that one of them had become homeless and another was shot. I went to my principal and asked why teachers are not informed and said I had a place in my home.

He looked at me but said nothing.

After school, I was informed that I was being transferred the next day to teach in a primary school. I never got to say goodbye to my students. I had never worked with primary students before. Though I did well, my heart wasn't in it. My mind never left the image of the boy who sobbed about aging out and then never returned to school.

I searched Eventbrite, which is an event app, looking for free networking events and trying to figure out what I would do next. Then I came across a woman named Kay Fittes. She was everywhere, at social events, Toastmasters, and community gatherings. She didn't know me well, but when I told her I wanted to do a TEDx talk, start a small business, found a nonprofit, and write and illustrate a picture book, she smiled and said, "Leila, you can do everything. Just not at the same time."

Something clicked. I spent an entire year trying to do it all. At the end of that year, I accomplished nothing. Then I pursued the TEDx. That's when focus became freedom. A few months later, I did the talk. The talk sparked a movement. Shortly after, House Bill 50 passed, giving foster youth in my state a home until age 21. Did I do that alone? No. It was a collaborative effort that required everyone's voice, I simply added mine. I often say we fail alone but succeed together.

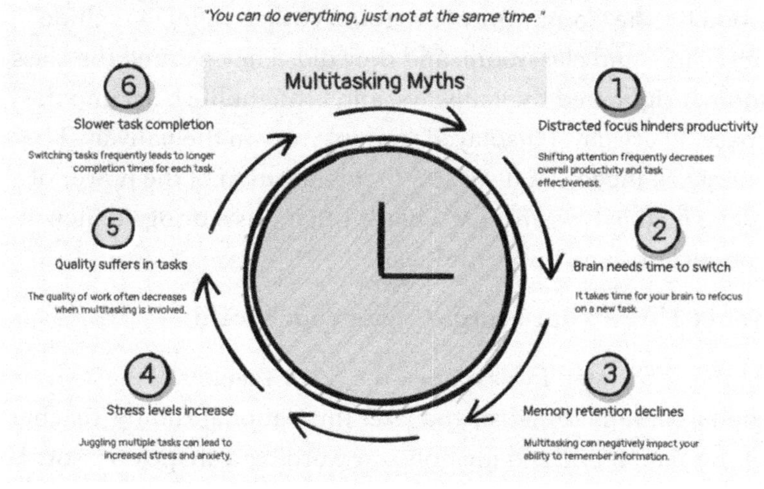

Tenet Two: Speak for the Opportunities You Desire

I applied for a new teaching job I found after the deadline had already passed, and was thrilled to get it. In my first week, a student in the back told me he looked me up online and saw my TEDx talk. He asked if I really cared about foster youth. "Would you do a speech about something you don't care about?" I asked. Heads went down. On the way out, several students in that class told me they were in foster care, in fact one third of the class.

At the end of the day, I drove home. My shirt felt wet. What happened? Did I drool all the way home? I looked in the rearview mirror and saw my face, puffy eyes, and red cheeks, and realized I had been crying in silence. In that moment, I thought, "I want to teach as if I were the State Teacher of the Year." Then I quickly corrected myself, "No, as if I were the National Teacher of the Year."

My classroom had lime-green walls cluttered with boxes stacked to the ceiling. I started cleaning. I looked online and found that the Hispanic Chamber of Commerce had a "Do

Good for the Community" program. I asked them to include my school and classroom, and they did. They painted the classroom, brightened the hallways, and brought life back into the space. Every day, I displayed student work in the hallway. The energy changed. That was my first realization of the power of social media. It wasn't just a platform; it was a bridge to new connections and opportunities.

Tenet Three: Your Words Create Your World

Three years later, I was named the State Teacher of the Year, then a National Finalist, and later the National Family Teacher of the Year. It amazed me how our words can shape our world. Now, I remind others to not only dress for the role you want but also speak for the opportunity you desire.

I had seen firsthand the power of language in shaping reality and outcomes.

I often hear people joke that they are "broke as a joke." It may sound harmless, but words carry weight. They shape how we think, how we act, and how others see what's possible for us.

When I won Family National Teacher of the Year, it came with $20,000 for my nonprofit.

Recently my non-profit now has formed partnerships with schools in Japan along with several other countries. We have interns from around the world applying to make a difference in their own communities. I remember when starting a nonprofit seemed like a far-fetched idea to others.

The picture book I dreamed of writing and illustrating? I submitted it to a publisher last week.

It all began with those three tenets and the realization that **what you speak, you eventually become.**

Chapter Summary

- Students aging out of the foster care system during their high school education, leaving them homeless and facing violence, pushed a hard reset of my priorities and focus.
- Focus changes everything; one TED Talk first, then the rest.
- Acting like "Teacher of the Year" preceded the titles, as language led action.
- Social media mobilized real help, including classroom repainting, creating a talk show, donations, and community partnership.
- Speaking for the opportunity shapes outcomes.

Tips

- Choose one priority for the next 90 days. Hold the rest for 'next.'
- Before posting or speaking, check your wording. Does it create the world you want?
- Use social media to mobilize specific help. Name the need and the desired outcome.
- Treat the space you work in as a message by keeping it clean, visible, and hopeful.

Reflection & Application

1. Which tenet do you need most right now. and what would acting on it look like this week?

2. Write one sentence you'll carry into your work like a banner (e.g., "Teach like I am Teacher of the Year").

3.W hat is one concrete, visible change you can make in your environment to shift energy?

4. Draft a single, focused ask you can make on social media to mobilize help for your current project.

5. Which words or jokes do you want to retire because they don't match the world you want to build?

BRIDGE TO CHAPTER 8

Mindset is the engine, but advocacy is the vehicle. Now, let's use your platform and voice to serve others and invite real change.

8

WHEN FRUSTRATION BECOMES FUEL

Some lessons never announce themselves; they arrive quietly through disappointment, through waiting, or through someone's small act of faith.

The Missed Moment

When I was invited to speak at a major venue in New York, I was elated. It felt like a dream opportunity, the kind you prepare your whole life for. I hired a photographer to capture the event hoping to use the photos in an article and share them online to extend the message beyond the room.

She arrived late, missing the opening of my talk. I tried not to show my frustration, telling myself to *just stay focused.*

Days passed with no word. A week later and still nothing. Ten days later, she finally sent a link.

I opened it expecting a polished set of images. Instead, it was a digital dump containing hundreds of unedited shots. They were blurry. Grainy. Distant. Heads cropped off. Not one captured the energy of the room. My eighth graders could've done better with their phones.

I wish I'd handed my phone to an attendee. I had paid $200 for proof of a moment that looked like it never happened.

I sat at my desk, staring at the folder, realizing the only story those photos told was one of carelessness. In a world where visibility is digital, that absence erased what had been a defining day. The disappointment was sharp, but beneath it something shifted.

The Rediscovery

I remembered the countless photos I'd taken of my students, showing their pride, their projects, and their faces lighting up in discovery. Those photos held a story and they had heart.

That memory pulled me back years earlier to when a newspaper reporter promised to visit my class and never showed up. When my students were crushed. One even remarked at the time, "If we had done something wrong, we'd be on the front page."

That day, I picked up a disposable camera and photographed their projects myself. It wasn't perfect, but it was something, and that something became everything.

I began documenting every project, every event, every win, big or small. Soon, I was writing grants that included photography equipment so students could learn alongside me. Eventually, their photos appeared in magazines and exhibitions alongside my writing.

None of it would've happened if that reporter had shown up. Years later, the same truth echoed again; in the digital world, if you don't tell your story it disappears.

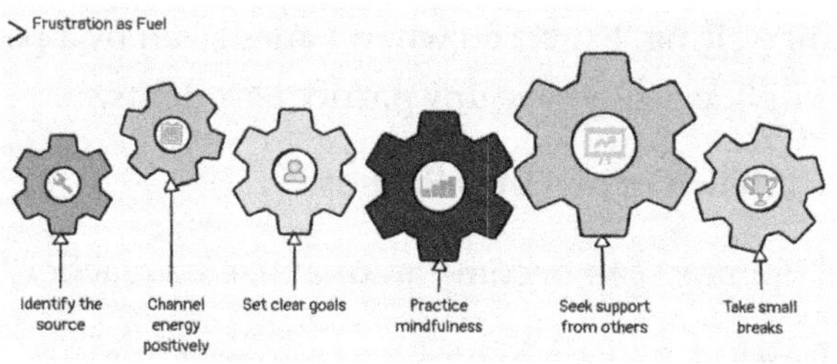

The Shift Point

That's when I stopped calling things failures. I began seeing them as processes of elimination and removing what didn't work to make room for what will.

When something doesn't go as planned, I now ask "*what's another way?*" Those four words change everything.

Early in my career, I used to wonder "why me?" whenever things went wrong. But "*why me?*" kept me stuck and unhappy. Instead, "*what's another way?*" makes me curious.

And curiosity opened every door that frustration had closed, both on stage and online.

The Hidden Gift

I once applied for a $3,500 grant that I poured my heart into. It was rejected.

Instead of giving up, I sent the same proposal to another donor. The only change? I added a zero. We won $35,000.

That moment reminded me that rejection is often redirection, and that visibility in any form requires persistence, not perfection. Imagine if I had waited for my English to be perfect before writing grant proposals. I might still be waiting. We can't wait for everything to be ideal; we work with what we have and make the most of what's available now. I've met people whose English is flawless, their only language, yet they came to me to learn grant writing. I succeed when I am driven by a passion to achieve, not because I have any particular talents.

How a Problem Turned into Purpose

A missed opening can become an unexpected teacher.

Moving forward, I've made photography part of my keynote work, and not as a backup but as an extension of my mission to give voice and visibility.

Eventually, I explored using a remote shutter, practiced, and learned to navigate the stage with ease. Now I manage both the clicker for my slides and the remote shutter, capturing action photos of myself on stage and with attendees who want pictures together after my keynote.

Each snapshot holds the energy of people learning and uniting in real time. Afterward, I send the photo gallery to the event planner as a gift, a thank-you they can share to promote next year's conference and celebrate their community.

Those photos often become the most-shared content from the event. They capture what words can't, showing people belonging, learning, and laughing together. It's how I reciprocate for the invite to serve as the keynote speaker.

Behind the Lens: A Speaker's View

People often ask how I manage to be both the keynote speaker and the event photographer. The answer is simple, I plan for it.

Before the event, I set up my gear so I can move freely and capture moments naturally. During breaks or after my session, I switch roles, documenting the energy I helped create.

Photography lets me extend the keynote and turn the spirit of the day into images that keep the story alive long after the applause fades. Each photo becomes a reflection of connection, which is the heartbeat of every event.

Reframing the Setback

Looking back, that disappointing experience in New York wasn't a failure at all. It was an invitation to reclaim what I already knew, that I could merge my eye for stories with my mission to serve.

Every missed opportunity reminded me that visibility isn't about control, it's about contribution. What I once saw as a loss became proof that authentic moments, online or off, carry the most impact.

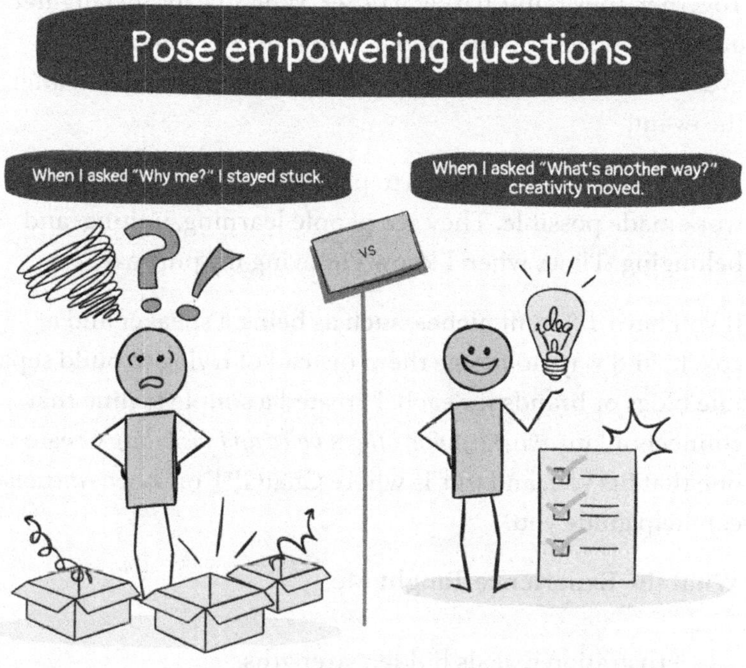

Making Sense of Two Roles

For a long time, I struggled to explain my dual identity as a keynote speaker and photographer. At first, it felt contradictory. I was often told to stick to one niche, to be either a photographer or a speaker. Remember how I said I don't like advice? I found a way to merge both.

I realized both serve the same mission to give voice and visibility.

Speaking gives voice, it helps people see possibilities. Photography gives visibility, it helps people see themselves in that possibility.

Together, they reinforce each other. When I capture laughter, engagement, and connection, I'm not just documenting an event, I'm connecting with attendees before, during and after the event!

When I return those photos to planners, they see what their work made possible. They see people learning, uniting, and belonging. That's when I know I'm living my purpose.

If you have different niches, such as being a speaker and a coach, find ways to merge them instead of trying to build separate blogs or brands for each. I created a simple tagline that connects all my work: *giving others voice and visibility.* Create one that fits you, and this is where ChatGPT or other AI tools can help guide you.

What the Experience Taught Me

- Frustration reveals hidden strengths.
- Mastery often hides in plain sight.
- Use what you have, the best tools are already in your hands.

- Gratitude connects us. Turning skill into a gift transforms service into a legacy.
- Visibility and generosity can coexist. You can shine and still make space for others to shine too.

Chapter Summary

- Disappointment often reveals the strength you've overlooked.
- You don't always need new tools, sometimes you just need to recognize your own.
- When your work becomes a gift, frustration becomes fulfillment.
- Visibility paired with service creates a lasting impact both on stage and online.

Tips

Treat your talents as service, not just hobbies for yourself and find ways to merge your work. Notice how I include poems throughout this book to explain certain ideas. I used to hide them, afraid they were silly or not good enough. Now, I see them as part of how I share my content. Readers can choose to read them or skip ahead, but they're woven into my way of connecting and communicating.

- Revisit old creative work—it holds evidence of skills you've already mastered.
- Keep your camera close; inspiration often hides between moments.
- When things fail, ask: *What ability is this reminding me I already have?*
- Share process, not perfection—your digital visibility grows through authenticity.

Just breathe when things don't go well.

Reflection & Application

1. What's one skill you've undervalued or taken for granted?

2. When did frustration help you rediscover a strength?

3. How can you use your creative talents to support others, online and off?

4. Who could benefit from the gifts you once dismissed as "just something I do"?

Bonus: Visibility in Action

When I don't bring my own camera gear, I make a point to meet the event photographer, ask for a few photos if I'm speaking in a breakout session, and offer a small gift card as a thank-you. I exchange contact information right away and follow up afterward. In the past, I would hand out my business card and never hear back. Photos from event photographers often never get posted, but a simple gesture of appreciation builds goodwill and can turn a single snapshot into a lasting collaboration. If you notice an event photographer, introduce yourself and do the same.

- If you're attending an event, whether as a speaker, sponsor, or participant, visibility isn't just about being seen. It's about how you connect, both in person and online.
- Connect on LinkedIn and follow up, saying for example *"Thank you for capturing the spirit of the event. I'd love to credit your photos when they're shared."*
- That one connection can open doors and expand visibility for both of you. And if no photographer is present, ask a fellow attendee to capture a few candid moments of you speaking, learning, or connecting.

- These aren't just for social media. They are reminders of contribution and community. Visibility works best when it's rooted in generosity. Honor the people behind the lens, and everyone shines a little brighter.

I never take selfies. Ever. I believe that if I can't ask for something small, like having someone take my photo, how will I ever ask for something big?

Once, while I was in Japan, I wanted to capture a photo of a beautiful building reflected in the water. Someone nearby offered to take a picture of me standing in front of it. Just as they were about to, another person ran over and said, "Oh no, let me take a photo of you both together!" By the time we finished, there were twelve people in the photo. I only wanted the building, but we all laughed so hard once everyone realized we weren't even together. Make time to connect with others in person or online.

Bridge to Chapter 9

Visibility begins by showing up with intention and making connections. The next chapter is about how to turn those connections into meaningful impact.

9

VISIBILITY THAT WORKS

Sometimes visibility doesn't roar, it whispers. It hides inside quiet moments, small posts, or even videos that almost no one sees.

The Two-Minute Video That Opened Doors

The first video I ever created lasted just two minutes. No script. No fancy gear. Just eagerness to learn and try something new.

It was made using Canva and created from real LinkedIn recommendation exchanges. I wasn't even in the video. I didn't say a thing.

It had fewer than ten views. And yet, that tiny clip brought me unexpected invitations to Canada, Thailand, and Cameroon.

That was the moment I understood that people aren't as interested in what you do as much as the transformation you create.

The Story Behind the Clip

Months earlier I attended the Global Speakers Summit Conference in Bali, just as a learner. I brought my camera to test what it felt like to travel with professional equipment, the weight, the logistics, the discipline of creating abroad.

The showcase began in TED-style, fifteen minutes allowed per speaker. Moments before the first speaker went on, she broke down in tears, trembling. Her country had been bombed that morning.

From the front row, instinct took over. I jumped to my feet and approached her. "What can I do? Would you like some water?" I asked. She shook her head, tears streaming, nose running, trying to steady her breath. She told me she had just learned that her country had been bombed. She wanted to give her talk first to get it over with and didn't want to wait until the end.

I pointed at my camera and said, "See that? I can do your photo shoot so you can share this moment with your family." Her eyes widened. She wiped her nose with the sleeve of her dress and asked, "Really?"

Then came the interruption. The next speaker, a man from South Africa who overheard, snapped his fingers for my attention, and said, "yeah, I want the same!" Snapping at me? I kept my cool. But I was displeased. I replied, "I'm not the event photographer!" He said, "Thanks," and walked away. I muttered to myself, "I'm not spending an entire afternoon doing extra work. I can take the photos, but I don't have to process them!"

Weeks later, I received a LinkedIn message from him. He asked if I had any good photos of him because the event photographer didn't. I processed one photo and sent it to see if he liked it. He loved it and asked if I had more. I replied by asking if he would be willing to write a recommendation.

That single exchange became the heartbeat of my little video. It was a short video about that experience. And that opened three international opportunities!

The Unexpected Reach

I used the recommendation to be creative in creating a video as a learning experiment using Canva. I stitched the photos together with captions and posted it to LinkedIn. No expectations. Only a handful of views.

But the right people saw it.

Within weeks, messages started arriving. "Would you photograph our event?" "Can you create a short video like that for us?" What's interesting is that the video had zero likes or comments on my LinkedIn. That's why I always say it's not the number of followers or likes that make the difference.

That small post reminded me that you don't need a crowd to create momentum. You just need alignment between your story and someone else's need.

That video landed me invites to Canada, Thailand and Cameroon! See for yourself how simple this promo is, and I didn't say a word!

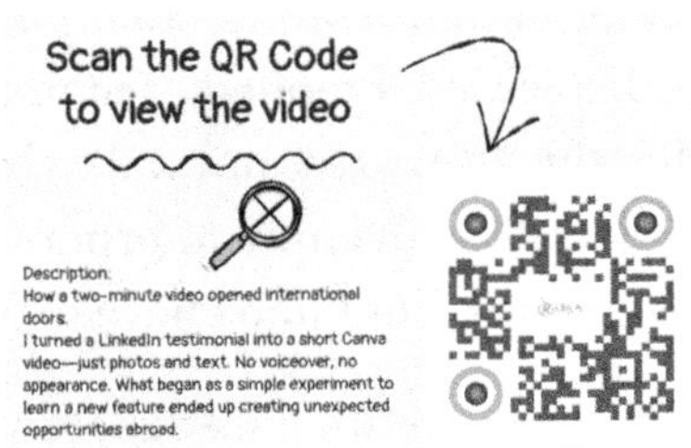

Scan the QR code or use the link above.

What That Moment Taught Me

1. Small doesn't mean unseen. Impact is measured in resonance, not views.

2. Visibility is service. When you show up generously, the right people notice.
3. Every post is a calling card. Someone is always watching quietly.
4. Consistency beats perfection. Steady presence builds trust faster than sporadic brilliance.
5. Your work speaks when you can't. Share it so opportunity has a way to find you.

Creative Ways to Showcase Your Work: Visibility doesn't live only in a feed or profile, it lives in how you share your story across mediums.

- Short Videos (1–2 minutes): Honest, no-frills recordings draw people in.
- Photo Galleries & Portfolios: Document milestones with captions and context.
- Carousel Posts/Slideshows: Turn lessons learned into a mini-guide or story.
- Live Talks & Micro-Webinars: Human presence builds real-time trust.
- Presentations & Slide Decks: Share visual summaries for easy connection.
- Written Stories & Blog Posts: Invite empathy with conversational storytelling.
- Testimonials & Case Studies: Let other voices validate your impact.
- Podcasts & Audio Snippets: Convey warmth and credibility in your own voice.
- Behind-the-Scenes Moments: Share prep, brainstorming, or outtakes.
- Collaboration Highlights: Celebrate joint wins and tag partners generously.

Chapter Summary

- Visibility doesn't require volume, it rewards authenticity.
- Quiet traction can become a lasting impact when it reaches the right audience.
- Service, not perfection, is the truest marker of value.
- Consistency creates trust and opportunity.
- Creative sharing multiplies visibility into legacy.

Tips

- Try using a new format, video, gallery, or story, to reach a fresh audience.
- Ask for a recommendation when they rave about your work.
- Document even your smallest projects. They may open the biggest doors.
- Share not only what you learned, but how you learned it.

Reflection & Application

1. What project of yours had quiet traction with small numbers but big impact?

2. Which creative format feels most natural for you to try next?

3. How could one act of generosity become a story worth sharing online?

4. What visibility habit could you practice weekly that feels sustainable?

5. Who can you ask today for a recommendation on your LinkedIn profile?

Bonus | Visibility Challenge

- Choose any small project, post, or act of generosity that you're proud of, no matter how small.
- Document it using one creative format above (even a phone photo or short text update).
- Pair it with a one-sentence about a lesson learned.
- Share it on LinkedIn or with a trusted peer.
- Make the ask for a recommendation.

Questions for your 'Visibility File'

- What worked unexpectedly in your experiment?
- Who reached out, and what did they see that you didn't?
- How could your story help someone else show up quietly?

If you complete the challenge and notice a result (big or subtle), let it feed your legacy. If you wish, share your outcome with the community or with me! The ripple may begin sooner than you think.

Bridge to Chapter 10

Visibility is always a gift and not a guarantee, but it begins when you choose to show up honestly and share your story your way.

10

FROM RED MARKS TO RESILIENCE

In my first college English course, we studied Shakespeare and I didn't understand a word of it. I was a non-native English speaker determined to master the language, so I lived in the library with a massive dictionary, looking up every unfamiliar word and trying to make sense of each sentence one at a time.

Trying to sound correct, I started using Shakespeare's words in my writing even though I didn't know how to say them. My papers came back covered in red marks, question marks, and notes on grammar, punctuation, and run-ons. My grades? Always a C.

Every writer remembers the moment their confidence met a red pen. Mine came early.

It was clear that English wasn't my first language. Spelling, grammar, and pronunciation tangled together. Even words that looked like cousins, like *tough, through, enough*, seemed to have nothing in common.

But I was determined to improve. To help myself remember pronunciation, I started writing short rhyming poems, not for grades, but to train my ear. That humble daily practice became key to mastery and my confidence.

Bringing Talent to the Table

Years later, that playful practice re-emerged when I became a speaker. I love a good cadence, alliteration, and funneling words into sequence. I wanted to experiment with creating videos, so I took one of my poems, used a mic as a prop and a swivel stool, and recorded a simple clip just to practice and learn how to do videos and learn more features within Canva.

Behind this Two-Minute Video

The video quickly shot past two thousand views. It was basic, shot on a stool with a ring light, featuring a Canva-generated backdrop and a non-functioning mic as a prop. A teleprompter app (Speakflow) kept me on track. It looked real even though it was all homemade.

No script. No fancy equipment. Just honest practice.

And it worked.

I received many kind direct messages on TikTok. What I realized was that I had brought up the "elephant in the room," a phrase in English meaning the issue everyone thinks about but doesn't talk about. I want event planners and everyone else to know that yes, I do have an accent. I'm well aware of it, and I did struggle with English, but I'm doing my best in the way I know how.

That short video had over 2,000 views. I never expected that kind of response, especially since some of my other videos barely reached nine views. I was simply exploring a new social media platform and learning as I went.

I also shared why I write poems. When people see them, they're sometimes surprised—"Wait, you do photography, you speak, and now you write poems? What's your niche?" My niche is that I communicate in different forms so my message can reach people who learn in different ways, and I encourage others to do the same.

Scan the QR code or use the link above.

What I Used for My First Video

- Swivel stool (for movement and angle)
- Ring light (for clarity)
- Canva background (visual cohesion)
- A broken mic as a prop
- Speakflow app (to help me stay on script)

When Visibility Meets Vulnerability

Our quirks become bridges. When you go visible, opinions follow. Some support and some sting. It is easy when the likes roll in and harder when criticism appears. Now if harsh feedback comes, I ask myself, "Is this real feedback or just noise?" If it helps me grow, I listen. If it distracts, I move on. Recently, a trailblazing presenter recounted how a commenter teased her for a lisp she did not even have. She paused, then answered, "Yes, I am the lady with the lisp." The label lost its sting. Not everyone will understand you, but confidence comes from staying rooted in your why as you continue to show up. When the comments come, anchor yourself in who you are and why you started. Respond with clarity and kindness if needed. Sometimes silence is strength. The more visible you become, the more vital it is to protect your peace. Your job is not to convince, it is to continue. **Key points to remember:**

- Anchor yourself in your why
- Listen to feedback that helps you grow
- Release the noise that distracts
- Respond with clarity and kindness when needed
- Let silence be strength when it serves you
- Protect your peace as visibility grows

Chapter Summary

- Expression invites response. Your strength lies in how you receive it.
- Authenticity outlasts approval.
- Every creative act, including writing, posting, and speaking, is an act of courage.
- Your story gains power when you stop editing it to please everyone.
- The more visible you become, the more important it is to stay grounded in your purpose.

Tips

Know that successful people are busy creating and making an impact. It is often the others who feel the need to put people down. That is who they are, and they are not your responsibility. Move on, move up, and move forward.

This behavior is often called **the crab mentality.** The idea comes from watching crabs in a bucket. When one tries to climb out, the others pull it back in, and no one gets free. The phrase is widely recognized in the Philippines, where it became a way to describe how people sometimes react when someone else begins to rise. The metaphor stayed because it is such an honest reflection of human behavior. Do not step into that story. Keep climbing. Those who spend their energy pulling others down stay exactly where they are.

- Practice matters more than perfection. Use new tools as playgrounds to try new things.
- Separate growth feedback from pure noise.
- Keep a "Praise Folder" for kind words on hard days.
- Re-read your story aloud for purpose, not only proofing.
- Remember that your visibility is for connection and service.

Reflection & Application

1. What feedback once silenced you, and what can it teach you now?

2. Are your posts seeking approval or alignment?

3. What part of your story do you still hide that could empower someone else?

4. How can you model steady confidence amid criticism?

5. What creative risk will you take this week simply for practice?

Bonus: Vulnerability into Visibility Challenge

- Pick something that once made you self-conscious, like an accent, a tech hiccup, or a creative quirk.
- Share a story or create something that celebrates it.

Publish it for your audience or yourself. Notice how your own perception shifts.

- Track small reactions, internal and external, in your "Visibility Journal" or "Praise Folder."

Bridge to Chapter 11

I've learned that visibility often begins long before we realize anyone is watching. A quiet post, a simple story, a reflection written at the end of a long day can travel farther than our most polished efforts. And when those small offerings land in the right hands, they create connections we could never orchestrate on our own. That's the part I want to show you next, how the smallest things we share build the bridges that carry us forward.

11

BEYOND THE SCREEN: TURN VISIBILITY INTO REAL IMPACT

Sometimes the most meaningful opportunities don't start in boardrooms or on big stages. They begin quietly with a post, a message, or a story that lands in the right inbox at the right moment. When I was still teaching, I often blogged about classroom challenges, stories about students, learning, and hope. I never knew who read them, but every so often a comment would appear: "I saw your post, and it stayed with me." Sometimes it was an invitation. Sometimes a resource. Sometimes just a simple word of encouragement. Those moments reminded me that visibility, when grounded in service, carries farther than we ever see.

Years later, that same pattern continued through my nonprofit, Parents2Partners. College students began reaching out eager to intern. They read something I wrote, like a short article or a story from my newsletter, and said my mission resonated with them. They were drawn not just to what I do, but why I do it. Visibility connects people who are aligned in purpose long before they ever meet in person. What struck me most was the kindness of their tone, formal, thoughtful, and sincere. They weren't just looking for experience, because they can get that anywhere. They were looking for belonging.

Many mentioned the photos, visuals, and stories in my newsletters and how they felt part of something just by reading. The same thing happens in my speaking and photography work. After events, I often receive messages months or even years later from attendees who remember something I said or wrote. They will tell me, "I heard you speak at a webinar, and I've been following your work since." Those moments remind me that what we share online is never wasted. A single story or post can open doors long after we've moved on.

Even when applying for speaking engagements, I notice that people from those organizations often view my profile afterward. That tells me my outreach made an impression. That is why I make it easy. I include everything someone might need in one place on my LinkedIn profile, videos, reels, testimonials, and media links. Few people will click around to multiple sections on a website, and everyone appreciates ease. Visibility isn't luck, it is design. You build it with intention, one small act of clarity at a time.

A Mini-Guide: Connecting Across Generations

Working across classrooms, conferences, and cultures taught me the crucial lesson that visibility isn't one-size-fits-all.

Even within a culture, each generation has its own rhythm, from the pace they read, the tone they trust, and the kind of stories that pull them in. When we understand that, our communication becomes more human and far more effective.

Gen Z, The Digital Natives (Born after 1997)

Gen Z grew up swiping before they could spell. They process information through movement, sound, and authenticity. If a message feels rehearsed, they scroll away in seconds.

How to Connect:

- Use short-form video (Reels, TikTok, YouTube Shorts) to show what you stand for in motion.
- Keep your tone honest and unpolished. They prefer a conversational tone of writing.
- Share small, teachable moments, such as what went right, what went wrong, and what you learned.
- Invite participation using polls, questions, or challenges to make them feel seen.

What Builds Trust: Honesty. Humor. Humanity. Make them feel part of the process and they'll become loyal advocates.

Millennials, The Purpose Seekers (Born 1981–1996)

Millennials are driven by meaning. They want to know the story behind what you do, not just the headline. They resonate with causes, collaboration, and creative freedom.

How to Connect

- Tell a story, but make it useful. Blend personal lessons with practical takeaways.
- Use visuals that feel lived-in, not staged; think candid photos or real workplace moments.
- Write as if you're talking to a peer over coffee, not giving a lecture.
- Highlight progress. Share your "in-the-making" stories.

What Builds Trust: Transparency. Purpose. Shared values. They appreciate leaders who admit what they're learning.

Gen X, The Bridge Builders (Born 1965–1980)

Gen Xers grew up before the internet but mastered it out of necessity. They value competence and consistency. They're often the decision-makers behind major opportunities and collaborations.

How to Connect:

Offer clarity and proof by showing results, not hype.

- Use articles, presentations, and data-backed posts to demonstrate expertise.
- Stay professional but approachable, using short paragraphs, clean visuals, and credible sources.
- Honor their time. Being concise content is a sign of respect.

What Builds Trust: Expertise. Efficiency. Consistency. Deliver on promises, and they'll keep returning.

Baby Boomers, The Relationship Builders (Born 1946–1964)

Boomers value relationships and reliability. They prefer genuine conversation to flashy trends and respond to professionalism and kindness that feels personal.

How to Connect:

- Lead with gratitude. Send handwritten notes or thoughtful messages stand out.
- Highlight long-term results, milestones, and impact stories.
- Invite them to contribute their experience, such as "what's one lesson you'd share with younger professionals?"
- Use email newsletters or in-person updates. They appreciate direct, curated communication.

What Builds Trust: Respect. Follow-through. Authentic appreciation.

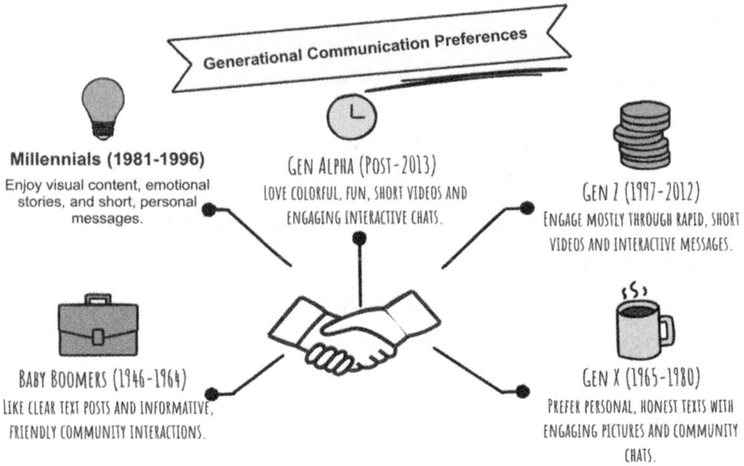

The Universal Rule: Connection Is About Empathy

The language of visibility may change with time, but the heart of it doesn't. Every person, no matter their age, wants to feel respected, understood, and valued.

Connection isn't about mastering an algorithm. It's about mastering attention, the kind that listens, not just looks.

If you can adapt your voice without losing your values, you will be able to bridge generations effortlessly.

Chapter Summary

- Visibility builds trust before conversation begins.
- Online presence is an invitation to connection, not a competition for attention.
- Automation doesn't replace authenticity, it sustains it.
- Understanding generational habits turns good content into a meaningful connection.

- The goal is not to be viral, it's to be valuable.

Reflection & Application

1. Think of one story or blog post that quietly opened a door for you. What made it connect?

2. What element of your digital presence (a post, photo, or video) best shows your purpose?

3. Which generation do you connect most naturally with, and which might you learn to reach better?

4. What one system or habit could make your visibility sustainable, not stressful?

5. Who might already be looking for you, and how can you make it easier for them to find you?

Bridge to Chapter 12

Visibility opens doors, but connection keeps them open. And sometimes all you need to begin is one simple message. We often underestimate how much we already know until we see someone light up because of what we share.

12

STOP BEING THE BEST-KEPT SECRET

One evening, during an online training session, I felt a spark to act before the session even ended. Without overthinking, I sent two direct messages to people I'd never met asking if they would like to become accountability partners so we could help each other apply what we learned. Both replied within minutes, enthusiastic, grateful, and ready to begin. They said they'd wanted to do something similar but didn't know how to start. Before the week ended, we were already meeting and putting ideas into practice.

That small act of just reaching out opened a door much bigger than I expected.

When You Reach Out, You Reach Up

The two partners couldn't have been more different. One was an established speaker with a strong following, the other was just beginning her speaking journey. At first, I assumed I'd learn more from them than I had to offer in return, but what unfolded surprised me.

I found myself sharing tools, systems, and strategies, things I'd learned through trial and error, not textbooks. They both called me very resourceful and thanked me for helping them organize, plan, and move forward. They weren't wrong. Resourcefulness had always been my strength. I just hadn't realized it was valuable.

One showed me how to launch a YouTube channel. The other taught me to check my spam folder for meeting links. Through that exchange, I discovered that people often see our light long before we do.

The Saturday Mastermind

Not long after, one of my accountability partners shared a quiet dream. "I hope to give a TEDx talk, maybe in five or ten years," he said. "Five or ten years?" I laughed. "Let's make that sooner." And just like that, our Saturday morning mastermind was born. We practiced, encouraged one another, and sent out applications. Within weeks, he landed an interview.

We both made videos to strengthen our submissions, and that little project became a turning point for me. I loved experimenting with new features and techniques while helping him reach his goal. Both accountability partners later wrote heartfelt recommendations on my LinkedIn profile, describing how our sessions helped them move forward. That's when it truly hit me that sometimes what you freely share becomes someone else's breakthrough.

The Real Reason We Stay Hidden

Most people don't mean to stay invisible. We just take our strengths for granted because they come naturally. We think "doesn't everyone know how to do this?" But what's easy for you might be extraordinary for someone else. The biggest reason we remain the best-kept secret is that we confuse humility with hiding.

Visibility isn't self-promotion, it's contribution. When you share what you know, you help others see what's possible for them.

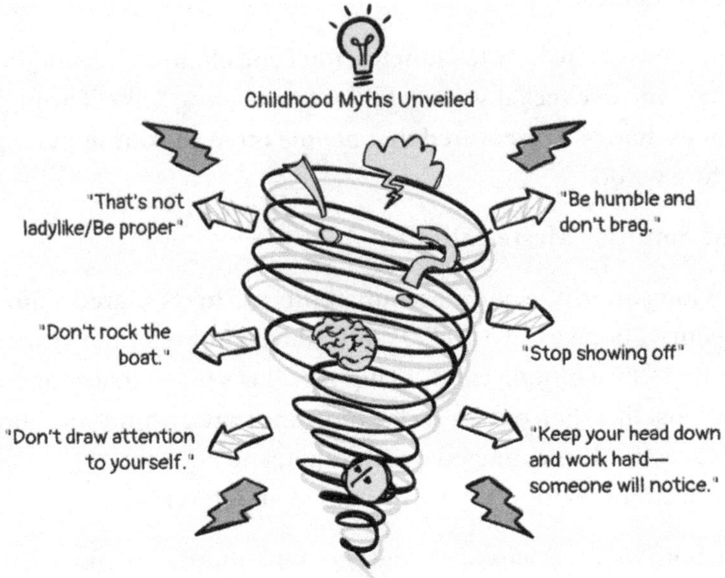

How to Stop Hiding and Start Showing Up

1. Reach out first. Be the one who starts the conversation.
2. Form small accountability circles. You don't need a big group. Two or three people with shared goals can build lasting momentum.
3. Teach what you're learning. Explaining something new helps you retain it and reveals your growing expertise.
4. Notice your ripple effect. When someone thanks you, listen carefully. That's your hidden strength speaking.

Chapter Summary

- Reaching out first is often the boldest form of visibility.
- Accountability turns learning into lasting change.
- Teaching others uncovers the value you already hold.
- Humility isn't hiding, service is how you shine.
- The best-kept secrets are people often those who underestimate themselves.

Reflection & Application

1. When have you acted before the moment passed and what changed because of it?
2. What do others thank you for that you barely notice?
3. Who could you invite into a circle of growth or accountability this month?
4. Which of your "everyday" skills might actually be your signature strength?
5. How can you make your expertise easier for others to find and benefit from?

Bridge to Chapter 13

As leadership gains momentum, sustaining your influence becomes the focus. In the next chapter, discover ways to keep your impact growing and your commitment strong. After discovering the impact of showing up and sharing your strengths, the next step is inviting others into the conversation. The right ask isn't about getting a favor, it's about sparking growth and collaboration.

13

ASK SO PEOPLE SAY YES

A single ask can change everything. This chapter is about making asks both online and in person that build trust, honor boundaries, and invite collaboration without pressure.

Why Asking Matters Sometimes asking feels harder than doing. We convince ourselves it's easier to figure it out alone, to stay quiet rather than do the uncomfortable work of reaching out. Yet every meaningful project I've built started with one brave ask.

How a Few Stretches Became a Space One day, my students walked into class and announced they were going to fail the quiz. These were gifted learners, straight-A students, but when they got their results, they were right. They did poorly. When I went over the answers, they were upset because they actually knew them all. Around that time, I had just completed my yoga certification. Before the next quiz, I decided to try something different. We took a few minutes to center ourselves, breathe deeply, and do a few stretches. They loved it and performed very well. Soon, they began asking to do those stretches more often. When I suggested yoga, they refused. "No, not yoga," they said. They just wanted those stretches.

I explained that is what we were doing. Once they understood that, their curiosity grew, and they wanted more of it. The challenge was the space. We had to move desks, drag furniture, and reset everything, which wasted time. Then one student said, "If only we had a room just for this." That simple comment sparked an idea to ask for a dedicated space just for yoga. Most of the fourth-floor wing was empty and filled with storage, mostly junk that had sat for decades.

The students made a clear, specific ask to the administrators. They only wanted the space. They were not asking for custodial help; they would move the items, clean, and organize everything themselves. Because they were clear, specific, and respectful in their request, the answer was yes. It was a reasonable ask, easy to approve, and it showed initiative. That is what I call making an ask with clarity: be specific and make it easy for others to say yes. My students and I used social media to enlist help from the community.

Making the ask helped us convert unused space into an in-house serene yoga studio.

A parent sewed the curtains, others donated paint and brought plants, and together we did the work. Making an ask online is just like doing it in person: be clear, share your reason, and explain how it benefits everyone. For example, by giving us the vacant room, students could make it better for the school, involve their peers, and help everyone feel more at ease to do well on tests.

From a Bold DM to Shared Momentum A single message can change everything. The Saturday Mastermind group I started showed me that asking with clarity creates movement. This chapter is about making asks that build trust, honor boundaries, and invite collaboration without pressure.

The Art of the Ask The Art of the Ask isn't about courage; it's about awareness. Many people think asking feels awkward, like they're imposing, but it's really about recognizing your own value and what you bring to the table. A lot of people hesitate to ask for help because they worry it will burden others. They say things like, "I wear too many hats," but then keep doing everything alone. However, asking isn't a sign of weakness—it's an act of connection. When you ask with purpose, you're communicating that you have something meaningful to offer in return. It shifts the exchange from need to reciprocity. A guest, collaborator, or mentor who gives their time might not expect payment but can still be thanked meaningfully through a handwritten note, a public acknowledgment on social media, or a thoughtful testimonial that highlights their impact. Genuine appreciation often carries more weight than money because it builds trust and strengthens future connections. That's what the Art of the Ask is really about: building relationships through mutual respect where both sides walk away feeling valued.

How to Ask So People Say Yes

1. Lead with purpose. Explain why it matters to you and to them. People say yes to meaning, not pressure.
2. Name the conditions that make it work. Whether it's space for yoga, help sewing curtains, or a partnership to serve as accountability pals—what's invisible becomes visible when you name it.
3. Offer reciprocity in advance. Bring value first, whether it is a resource, introduction, or insight. You're building a relationship, not bargaining.
4. Make saying "yes" easy. One link. Clear next steps. Simple choices.
5. Confirm understanding. Summarize the agreement in writing. Clarity prevents disappointment.
6. Follow through with gratitude. Close the loop by sharing results and saying thank you like you mean it.

Why Your "Ask" Matters Online or offline, most people fail at asking not because they're unworthy but because they're unclear. When you ask for support, clarity is your currency.

Here's what I tell my interns and coaching clients:

1. Lead with purpose. Before you ask, answer why this matters not just to you but to the person you're asking.
2. Be specific. "Can you help me?" is vague. "Would you be willing to review my one-page proposal by Friday?" is actionable.
3. Show credibility. People say yes when they know who you are. That's why a complete profile isn't vanity—it's trust.
4. Ask once and ask well. You don't need to chase or plead. A clear, respectful ask speaks louder than multiple reminders.

Online Etiquette That Builds Trust Professional etiquette online is not about being formal. People remember how you make them feel, even in a comment section. Your tone, timing, and attention matter more than perfect polish. I never worry much about grammar—you can always use tools like QuillBot or Grammarly for that. What I focus on is how my words will land.

Here's what builds quiet credibility:

1. **Reply when you can.** You don't have to respond to every comment, but try to reply to some. Acknowledgment shows appreciation. A simple "thank you for sharing that" or "I hadn't thought of it that way" can start a conversation that lasts beyond one post. Engagement is a two-way street.
2. **Respect DMs.** LinkedIn messages aren't text messages. You don't need to reply instantly. If someone doesn't reply to you, it doesn't mean they're ignoring you; people work, travel, live. If it's important, follow up politely once after a few days, then let it go.
3. **Mind the tag.** Tagging can build a connection or create clutter. Only tag people who are directly related to your post, and no more than three or four. Over-tagging feels like shouting in a quiet room. Tagging should never be used for attention—it's a form of invitation.
4. **Give credit.** If you quote, share, or use someone's idea, mention them. It's not just courteous; it's professional integrity. Generosity online travels fast. The people you credit often remember it long after the post fades.

Pro Tip If you wouldn't say it in a meeting or on stage, don't post it. Professional visibility should feel like an extension of your real-world presence.

Questions Worth Asking

- Would I say this face-to-face?
- Did I make space for others to speak?
- Do my words build trust or just noise?

Example

Vague Ask: "Hey, would you be interested in collaborating sometime?"

Clear Ask: "I loved your post about community outreach. My students are launching a service project, and I'd like to invite you as a virtual guest. We record on Wednesdays. Would you be open to joining one of our sessions this month?"

When Asking Feels Hard If asking feels uncomfortable, remember that most people like helping. They just need a reason to believe their effort will matter. Your job is to give them that reason. When you make an ask from a place of respect and purpose, it's not a favor—it's an invitation.

What Not to Do When Reaching Out Most people don't mean to come across the wrong way online. They just forget there's a real person on the other side of the message. A bad outreach doesn't make you unprofessional; it just means you haven't learned the rhythm of connection yet.

So let's make it simple.

1. **Don't copy and paste.** You know that message that starts with, "Hi, I came across your profile and..."? Everyone's seen it. Everyone's ignored it. If you want to connect, start like a human. Mention something specific about them and keep it short. Avoid flattery followed by a sales pitch. I have never bought a service or product from those kinds of direct messages. I want

to know the person well before I engage. Example: "I saw your post about teacher burnout. The part about boundaries really stayed with me." Real, specific, and sincere.

2. **Don't pitch in the first message.** Nothing ends a conversation faster than, "I can help you grow your business—book a call!" People connect to learn, not to buy. Let your first message build trust. If your work is valuable, people will find their way to you.
3. **Don't apologize for reaching out.** Messages that start with "Sorry to bother you" or "I know you're busy but..." instantly lower your presence. You're not a bother. You're a professional starting a conversation. Lead with respect, not apology. Instead of saying "sorry to take your time," try "thank you for taking a moment to read this." Confidence changes the tone.
4. **Don't forget context.** If you met someone at a conference or event, remind them. People remember moments better than names. Example: "We met at the HighLevel Conference—you shared great insight about automation. I wanted to follow up on one thing you said about simplifying systems." When you include context, you make it easy for people to place you and reply. Never write as if you know someone or assume they should know you. It comes across as irritating, and word gets around quickly.
5. **Don't leave your profile empty.** Reaching out without a filled-in profile is like showing up to a job interview without a résumé. People will look at your photo, headline, and About section before deciding whether to respond. Before you send your next message, make sure your profile clearly tells your story.

How to Turn "Don't" into "Do"

Many people send long or generic messages that sound like they were copied and pasted. A better approach is to write two or three short sentences that sound like you. Instead of leading with a sales pitch, begin with a question or shared interest. Replace over-apologies with gratitude or curiosity, and if you're reaching out after an event or online connection, remind the person where you met or what you discussed.

Before hitting send, take a moment to check your profile. An incomplete profile can close doors before you even start. Update your headline, About section, and photo so your outreach feels trustworthy and complete. Clear, warm communication paired with a strong profile helps people say yes more often.

Chapter Summary

- A few yoga stretches turned into a program because we asked for what we needed to make it repeatable.
- Reaching out first transforms learning into momentum.
- Clarity at the start is kindness at the end.
- Give yourself the advantage with a complete profile.

Questions Worth Asking Yourself When Reaching Out

- Would I reply to this message?
- Does my message sound like a person or a pitch?
- Does this message build curiosity or close the door?

Reflection & Application

1. What would make your current effort sustainable, your version of "a dedicated yoga room"? Ask for that.

2. Who could you invite into a two- or three-person accountability circle this month?
3. What value can you offer before making your next ask?
4. Rewrite one pending request to be purpose-led, clear, and reciprocal.

"Ask Practice" & Challenge

- Choose one real-life situation where you need support (a project, resource, or connection).
- Draft your ask using the five steps above.
- Share it with a peer, mentor, or group to collect feedback.
- Notice what felt the hardest and what got easier after trying.
- Celebrate both the yeses and the clarity that comes from a "not this time."

BRIDGE TO CHAPTER 14 A CLEAR ASK EARNS A STRONG YES. NEXT, we'll harness this collective power to turn yeses into collaborations that last. Learn how to keep the conversation alive without chasing—and how to let shared wins speak louder than self-promotion.

14

CONVERT CONNECTION INTO COLLABORATION

Some people wait for luck.

I've learned that luck often shows up after you've done the work. **Luck**, after all, is Labor Under Correct Knowledge.

Visibility opens doors, but collaboration keeps them open. The real difference between a one-time "yes" and a lasting partnership lies in what you do after the first connection. You're never unlucky, just unfocused.

Collaboration in Action: Chow & Tell, Leadership at the Table

During the pandemic, my students craved real-world skills. They wanted to learn their way around a kitchen. Their idea sparked the creation of "Chow & Tell," a student-hosted television cooking show.

The guests that were invited, however, weren't chosen for their cooking skills. Instead, each guest was a local leader, educator or community builder. They chose role models who could share stories from their own journeys, about their professions, and lessons learned beyond recipes. Each visit became as much about life and leadership as it was about making a meal.

Partnership here involved:
students, the filming crew, guest speaker, photographer, school leaders (who provided access to the room), and parents.

With the help of our local public television partner, episodes were filmed and produced. For each segment, I reached out personally, sometimes to community figures, sometimes to state leaders like Paolo DeMaria, Ohio's Superintendent of Public Instruction, whom I contacted via X (Twitter). Others responded to the invitations I sent through LinkedIn.

We also invited the local newspaper and a photographer, who generously gifted us a full photo archive capturing the richness of one episode and the guest.

The impact? Students not only learned kitchen basics, they heard about perseverance, education, and leadership from real people living their dream career paths. Our show became a hub where community, curiosity, and courage came together, all from sending one invitation at a time.

Use This "Ask" Template for Your Project:

"We would love to invite you to be a guest on our [show/event/project]. Would you be willing to support our program by sharing your story and expertise with our students?"

- Personalize by adding how their journey or leadership would inspire your group.
- Offer context, highlight your goal, your students' curiosity, or your community focus.
- Keep it direct, warm, and purposeful.

Reader Reflection:

- Who in your community could share a story, not just a skill?
- Which leader's journey might encourage your community to dream bigger?
- Draft your own version of the invitation and send it this week.

When a Simple Post Sparks Real Collaboration

A few years ago, I wrote a short post about my students hosting a TV talk show. It wasn't a request or a pitch, I simply wanted to celebrate their creativity.

Within days, local professionals began commenting and messaging me. They hadn't known about the project and wanted to visit the school to speak with my students. When they arrived, they already understood our mission, our goals, and why it mattered. They didn't need convincing because they were already invested.

Those visits transformed the tone of our classroom. Guests shared their career stories, my students lit up, and before leaving the visitors asked if they could return. That's when I understood what real collaboration looks like, it starts by putting your work where discovery can happen.

Create Your Own Luck

I don't believe in waiting to be found, I believe in working to **be findable.**

When I want to collaborate with an organization, I don't sit back and hope. If I see an event that aligns with my message, even if there's no listed contact or application, I find a way to reach out directly.

A short message can open a door. "I love the work your team is doing. Could you share how to be considered for future opportunities?" A note that takes two minutes to write has opened more doors than any cold application. I do my homework first. I learn about the organization, follow members, comment on their posts, and then ask to connect and explore how we might partner. There is no flattery about their profile, and I never ask them to look at anything. Too often, I receive long direct messages filled with links from people who claim they can improve my business without knowing what I do, then ask me to review their portfolio. Social media is meant to connect people, not waste their time scrolling through sales pitches.

When they respond, I make it easy to say yes. That's how I've landed collaborations and paid engagements that started as small exchanges.

A critical element of your email is the signature. It could (optional) include your website, photo, a flyer or one-page sheet about your work, and contact information. While you make these available, they should feel like an option, not an obligation. I include my demo reel as a YouTube link in my signature, and within a few days, I gained a lot of views simply because people were curious. I use WiseStamp and stick with the free version. You do not need to spend much money. It is not true that you must spend money to make money. Do what makes sense and never go beyond your means in the name of hope.

Luck doesn't wait, it's built.

What Collaboration Really Requires

True collaboration isn't about charm or flattery. I believe it entails **clarity, reciprocity, and follow-through.** Too often, people confuse flattery for connection. They send long messages full of praise, followed by a sales offer. That's not collaboration; that's a cold call in disguise.

The partnerships that last are built on shared purpose, like the financial literacy expert who volunteered to speak to my students. He didn't come for exposure; he came to serve. Before his visit, I asked how we could thank him, but he insisted he was just happy to help.

I guided my students to write thank-you notes, design a banner, and I posted about his visit online. That simple act of appreciation turned a one-time favor into a lasting partnership.

Sincere gratitude multiplies impact.

The Power of Reciprocity

People often ask me to do a photo shoot in exchange for giving me "exposure." It usually sounds like "I just need a few photos of me on stage, I'll tag you on LinkedIn!"

Requests like that happen often to people in creative fields. Many people mean well but the unseen hours don't fit inside a tag. For example, the uncredited labor of charging batteries, packing gear, setting up lights, traveling, and doing editing long after the event ends. Whether it's in person or online, it's best to avoid making those kinds of asks. If you're on the other end, pause before saying yes. It sends the message that your talent is not valuable enough to pay for.

In that case, refrain and save your time. I used to think making sacrifices for others showed appreciation, but often it only meant I didn't value my own work. Others were happy to take. I used to offer free services hoping for visibility, but many came back asking for more free work—and even told me how much they had paid someone else, were unhappy with the results, and still wanted me to do it for free. You can't feed your family exposure or visibility.

Some people truly can't afford professional services, and that's understandable. They can still show appreciation in meaningful ways. However, others act broke by asking for free work, and the next day they're posting about flying first class.

That's why I now set clear expectations up front. It keeps both sides aligned and protects relationships. Clarity early is kindness later. Don't barter your hard work; doing labor in exchange for exposure loses its shine fast because it's not a real partnership.

Even when someone volunteers their time, reciprocity still matters. Gratitude builds momentum. Visibility, acknowledgment, and respect are forms of currency too. Someone who truly values your craft doesn't get to define its worth, you do.

That's why it's okay to take a moment before you reply. Think about your values, your time, and what feels fair. You can always answer later, with clarity and confidence gained from reflection. Remember that clarity doesn't just open doors, it also protects your work, online and off.

Collaboration is not about bartering, it's about reciprocity. Bartering looks like "I'll do this if you do that." Reciprocity says "let's make this work well for both of us."

The 3 Cs of Lasting Collaboration

1. Communicate with Clarity: Say what you mean, name your needs, and invite others into the why.

2. Connect with Curiosity: Listen to learn, not to reply. Genuine interest builds genuine trust.

3. Collaborate with Consistency: Follow through, celebrate others' wins, and nurture relationships long after the first yes.

When these three align, opportunities don't just grow, they multiply. This is how visibility turns into collaboration.

When Collaboration Leads to Lasting Relationships

The most powerful partnerships I've built didn't end after one project. They grew because both sides invested in people, not transactions.

When I speak or photograph for an organization, I ask "what would make this easier for you?" Then I deliver more than promised; clear communication, prompt replies, and small touches that simplify their work. That's what turns a one-time invitation into an ongoing relationship. That's why I'm invited back.

Chapter Summary

- Luck isn't random. You are not unlucky, just unfocused, trying to do too many things at once.
- You don't wait for collaboration. You create it through clarity and care.
- Flattery isn't connection but follow-through is.
- Reciprocity sustains partnerships, while bartering drains them.
- The best collaborations are built on respect.

Tips for Turning Interest into Collaboration

Make the first move. Reach out clearly and without expectation.

- Give them something real to respond to. Include a short intro and visible proof of your work.
- Keep communication human. Write as you'd talk in person.
- Set boundaries early. Clarity creates trust.
- Give back by thanking them and/or publicly acknowledging their contribution. It costs little and means everything.

Reflection & Application

4. What opportunity could you create this week instead of waiting for one to happen?

5. How can you make yourself findable, not just visible?

6. What small gesture of gratitude could strengthen a relationship?

7. Where might you replace bartering with real reciprocity?

Bridge to Chapter 15

Collaboration thrives on clarity, but relationships deepen when others begin to speak for you. The next chapter explores how to let your work echo through the voices of those you've impacted, showing how to invite others to share and amplify your story to turn visibility into collective momentum.

15

LET OTHERS BRAG FOR YOU

Collaboration opens doors, and recommendations and testimonials keep them open wide. Once you invite others to share their experience of you, visibility multiplies organically and credibility grows over time. Here, we'll explore how letting others tell your story can unlock opportunities you might never reach alone.

The Power of Recommendations

The first time someone wrote me a recommendation, I paused. She described qualities I hadn't noticed in myself, such as the way I listen, how I follow through, and how I make people feel capable.

Reading those words, I realized recommendations do more than validate skill, they also reveal how our work shows up in the lives of others.

A few years ago, after attending a webinar I loved, I reached out to two attendees I'd never met to ask if they wanted to be accountability partners to apply what we'd learned. One was a successful entrepreneur with over 45,000 LinkedIn followers. We agreed to trade a half hour each to help each other.

When it was my turn, he asked how I'd landed international speaking engagements. When it was his turn, I asked what all those followers had done for him.

"Nothing," he said, smiling. "But my recommendations? That's where 90% of my business comes from." That stopped me cold. He looked at my profile and said, "Leila, it's strong, but you have zero recommendations. You're invisible where it matters most."

He was right. Though I had received many thank-you notes and praise, I'd never asked anyone to make those words public.

So I began to ask. To my surprise, it worked!

Asking for Recommendations and Multiplying Their Value

Now, after every keynote, workshop, or project, when someone compliments my work, I gently ask if they would be willing to write that as a short recommendation on LinkedIn.

When they post, I ask permission to copy the same text to my eSpeakers profile. That platform verifies the recommendation and boosts my SEO, doubling my reach.

I also highlight key quotes on my website, along with related talks or projects. Each page carries its own proof of impact.

Expanding visibility requires less effort than shouting louder. It was about letting others echo the truth of my work.

Reciprocating Generously

A recommendation is a currency, but also an act of kindness.

I make a habit of writing thoughtful recommendations for others, sometimes even composing poems about them.

Many leaders and colleagues in the speaking community have been honored through my poetic recommendations. I take the time to study their websites and craft testimonials with SEO in mind.

One leader loved their poem so much that they turned it into a video reel for their online presence.

Take the time to write recommendations that others are happy to post so it elevates them, showcases their skills, and naturally strengthens your relationship.

Tips for Letting Others Brag for You

- Ask while the moment is fresh.
- Personalize your request by mentioning what stood out in their feedback.
- Double your reach by posting testimonials on LinkedIn and your website. If you are a speaker, copy and paste them on eSpeakers.
- Reciprocate by writing one or two recommendations each month for those who have supported you.
- Keep a "praise folder" of kind words you have received to revisit and use later.

Chapter Summary

- Recommendations are a powerful form of social proof and validation.
- Asking for recommendations honors others' words and strengthens your reputation.
- Sharing testimonials across platforms multiplies your impact and visibility.
- Giving recommendations generously builds goodwill and networks.

- Gratitude and recognition are among your strongest SEO tools.

Reflection & Application

1. Who could you ask for a recommendation this week?

2. How might you turn thank-you messages into public testimonials?

3. What words would you love others to use when describing your work?

4. Who deserves your thoughtful recommendation today?

5. How can generosity through testimonials become part of your brand?

Bridge to Chapter 16

Your reputation grows not by chance but by intentional alignment. Next, learn how to build lasting relationships that are anchored in clarity, reciprocity, and genuine connection in order to expand your influence powerfully.

16

TURN CRITICISM INTO YOUR CALLING CARD

Having anchored yourself in gratitude and resilience, you are ready to transform one of the hardest parts of visibility, criticism, into something that fuels your growth and authenticity. This chapter explores how to claim your story, turn criticism into a source of strength, and use it as a powerful tool for connection and credibility.

When Criticism Turns to Strength

The first time I saw someone mocked online, it wasn't a stranger, it was a speaker I admired.

At a marketing conference, a dynamic presenter took the stage. She was brilliant, had sharp slides, amazing delivery, and genuine insight.

Later, she told us what no one watching the event would have known, that someone had commented on one of her videos to say "how can you be doing these videos when you have a lisp?"

She did not have a lisp!

That single remark could have unraveled everything, her voice, her confidence, her self-worth. But instead of hiding, she made a brave choice and she owned it. She smiled and replied publicly, "yes, I'm the lady with the lisp." Then she said something unforgettable, "I am the one on stage, not my critics."

She made that part of her story and called it **Embracing Your Weird**. That choice turned potential shame into an unmistakable strength.

When the Comment Hits Close to Home

Her story reminded me of an experience from my own teaching days.

I regularly helped fellow teachers translate letters for families who were newcomers and didn't speak English yet, carefully typing and formatting bilingual versions on school letterhead. I did this on my own time because I felt the students and their families deserved clear communication and I wanted to bring value to my colleagues.

One afternoon, an email meant for someone else landed in my inbox. It was from a teacher I had been volunteering to help, and it was mocking me. "Is she even speaking *our* English?" I read that and I was crushed. After what I had done, give my personal time for translating all of her communication to families?

For a long time, I wondered if I had done too much, and eventually resolved that I hadn't. It's my brand to give my best and bring value everywhere I go. Her "brand" is having a lack of regard toward others. Friends often urged me to stop spending my weekends translating her documents. I chose to continue and acted as if I never saw her comment. At first, I did it for her. Later, I did it for the families.

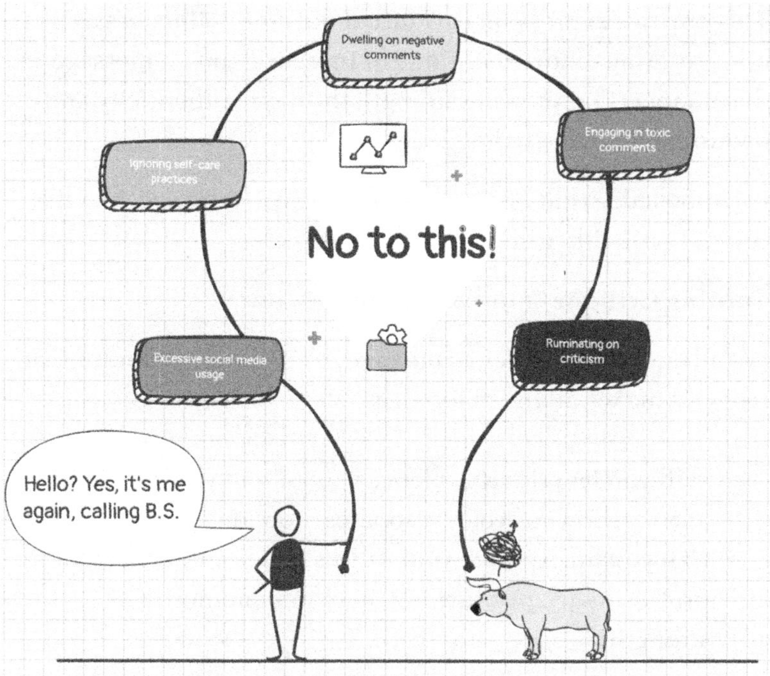

Instead of ruminating on the bull, I choose to graze on gratitude.

Owning Your Story Creatively

To lean into my own "weird," I created a video and a poem that shared my journey with words that don't follow a pattern, the very challenge I faced learning English as a non-native speaker. I wrote poems to help me remember pronunciation endings after listening carefully to how they were actually said.

The video openly calls out that I don't speak English as a native language, explains why I have an accent, and shares the struggle of navigating this challenge alone. But it's colored by humor, acceptance, and a declaration that no matter what, I'm owning my voice, and nothing about my speaking will get to me (not too much anyway).

A QR code in this book links to that video, inviting readers to see the vulnerability, humor, and resilience behind the voice.

This creative expression isn't just about storytelling; it's a powerful way to turn a critique or insecurity into a message that connects by showing strength through authenticity and inviting their own challenges.

I acknowledge that I have an accent I cannot change, and if I could, I probably would have by now.

Turning Critique Into Your Differentiator

We all encounter critics, some loud, some hidden. But how we respond makes all the difference.

- Will you let criticism silence you, or will you reclaim it as a reason your voice resonates more deeply?
- Can you incorporate your quirks into your personal or professional story, turning them into memorable strengths?

Sometimes your most visible imperfection becomes the credential people trust.

What if your next "flaw" became the story everyone wants to hear?

They Talk, You Build 💪

They hide behind a screen so small,
throw words that mean nothing at all.

They never show up, never create,
just wait to judge, to scroll, to hate.

But while they type, you move ahead—
your dream alive, their words long dead.

Your focus strong, your heart still true—
they talk a lot, but not like you.

Because change is made by those who show,
who dare to speak, who choose to grow.

Keep building light—let them complain.
You rise again while they remain. ⭐

Leila Kubesch

How to Use Criticism as a Signature

- Pause before reacting and ask, "is this noise or genuine feedback?"
- Name and own your differences. Don't shrink from what makes you unique.
- Share your story of resilience openly, making criticism part of your origin story.
- Use critique as fuel to clarify your strengths and deepen your connection.

Tips for Turning Criticism into Strength

- Integrate your "weird" or differences into your bio or brand narrative.
- Reflect on feedback and list the strengths you've demonstrated in handling it.
- Frame criticism moments as opportunities to show authenticity.
- Offer empathy and encouragement to others facing similar challenges.

Chapter Summary

- Criticism met with courage becomes credibility.

- Your response shapes how others perceive you.
- Owning your vulnerabilities can turn them into strengths.
- Feedback is a powerful storytelling tool.
- You control your narrative. What was once intended to damage can become design.

Why This Matters Your story will echo far beyond you. It helps others see possibilities, inspires courage, and creates a community that uplifts rather than silences. When you let others hear how you've turned critique into power, you build not just visibility, but legacy.

Reflection & Application

1. What criticism (public or private) still echoes in your mind?
2. How might you reframe it into a story of courage or humor?
3. Who do you know who has made a perceived imperfection their defining asset?
4. What narrative in your story needs rewriting, from wound to wisdom?

Bonus Challenge: Now it's your turn to Share Your Strength

Invite yourself to reframe a piece of criticism or a challenge you've faced into your "calling card", a story that showcases your resilience, growth, and unique power.

Use these prompts to craft your narrative:

- What was the criticism or setback that stung you the most?
- How did it impact your confidence or your story at first?

- What choice did you make to own or reframe that challenge?
- How has that decision shaped your voice, presence, or leadership today?
- What message would you want to share with others facing similar criticism?

Share your story!

Post your signature story on social media or your blog. Tag me if you feel comfortable, I'd love to celebrate your courage and resilience!

Bridge to Chapter 17

Embracing criticism is part of your visibility journey, and protecting your well-being is what makes that journey sustainable. What comes next is a simple story that reminded me how stress can cloud your thinking and how a tiny shift, the kind that helps on LinkedIn and in life, can restore clarity.

17

THE POWER OF SIDEWAYS DOORS: TINY SHIFTS THAT UNLOCK BIG WINS

I was supposed to attend a conference in New Jersey. Then the day before, my flight was canceled. Not delayed. Canceled. I let the organizers know, then called Embassy Suites hotel to cancel my room.

The man on the phone told me I wasn't eligible for a refund. I mentioned their twenty four hours in advance. He corrected me with, "*Madam, it is twenty thrrree hours and thirrrty minutes.*"

I explained that I had just found out and offered to show proof and asked for the manager. He told me he was the manager and that there was nobody else I could talk to. Perhaps he owned the entire hotel chain. He kept repeating the same line about the policy and I was getting frustrated.

I was about to hang up when he added the most ludicrous comment, "*You can come back anotherrrr time.*"

Why would I ever come back to a city I had no business visiting? I had just read that New Jersey had the highest rate of unhappy people. I was already unhappy and I wasn't even there yet.

Then I paused.

"*Wait, I could come back another day*?" I asked.

"*Of courrrse,*" he said.

"*I'd like to move it to two days later then.*"

"*Yes, madam, happy to help*" And he sent me the new reservation.

I hung up, called right back, and a different person answered. I told her I wanted to cancel my reservation.

"M*y pleasure,*" she said. "*Anything else for you today*?"

I asked for a cancellation confirmation.

"My pleasure," she said.

I stood there amazed at how absurd the whole thing was.

Why am I sharing this story?

The hotel wasn't the point. The dance around the "policy" was the point. It reminded me that sometimes the only way forward is sideways. A tiny shift. A different doorway. A different person. And suddenly the thing that felt impossible becomes effortless.

That same sideways-door hack is exactly how LinkedIn works.

When you post something that needs a link on LinkedIn, like a webinar or anything that makes members exit the platform, LinkedIn doesn't like it. When I say LinkedIn "doesn't like it," here's what I mean:

When a post includes a link that pulls people off the platform, LinkedIn quietly lowers how many people see it. It doesn't delete it or block it, it just shows it to fewer people. Your post doesn't travel as far, and fewer eyes land on it.

That's why the sideways-door works.

- Post first with no link or the Call to Action.
- Then return seconds later and edit the post.
- Add the CTA or the link right into it.

People sometimes put the CTA in the comments, which works, but editing the post keeps everything clean and easy to find.

The whole thing takes a moment. And suddenly the door that was locked isn't.

A calm mind sees options a stressed mind misses.

And if that hotel moment showed how sideways thinking works, the same is true for all of us. Rest fuels creativity. Science backs it up, stress blocks ideas, rest brings them back. Wellness shapes how we think and create.

Why Sustaining Well-Being Matters

Growing your visibility and influence demands internal care. Without nurturing your physical, emotional, and mental health, the shine you build can fade quickly.

Sustaining well-being is about:

- Building consistent restorative self-care habits.
- Cultivating a mindset of rest as part of growth, not guilt.
- Creating a support system that encourages balance.

My Daily Rituals to Keep Visible and Grounded

I start and end each day with a list of what I'm grateful for. This daily anchor grounds me and gives my mind a positive dock to return to. When I can't think clearly or the pressure mounts, that gratitude list reminds me of the good, nothing is too small.

I remind myself that no small mind shall squash the big things I strive to do.

Other rituals include mindful walking, brief meditation, and maintaining digital boundaries to avoid overload. I focus on big goals, not small tasks.

Building Energy Rituals That Stick

• Morning gratitude or intention-setting.

• Movement, like walking, stretching, or dancing, to awaken and restore.

• Scheduled breaks for disconnecting from devices and social media.

• Journaling your wins and challenges to process and reflect.

• Saying "no" strategically to protect focus and prevent becoming overwhelmed.

The Balance Mindset

Your worth isn't measured by how busy you are or your number of followers. Rest is a powerful part of growth, not its enemy. When you lean into cycles of activity and recovery, you create sustainable energy that lights the way for others as well.

Chapter Summary

• Sustained visibility requires sustained well-being.

• Rest and self-care fuel your growth and creativity.

• Wellness strengthens creativity and helps you navigate both social media and daily stresses with more clarity.

• Small sideways shifts like editing a post or navigating a rigid policy become easier when your mind is rested and steady.

• Daily rituals anchor your energy so you can remain visible without losing yourself.

• Boundaries empower you to say yes to what matters most.

- Your well-being is central to maintaining your capacity to continue creating meaningful change for yourself and others.

Reflection & Application

1. What are your current daily rituals for self-care and energy?
2. Which "must-do" can you swap out for a "must-rest" without guilt?
3. How does your current work-life balance support or hinder your visibility goals?
4. Which boundaries would make your creative or professional life healthier?
5. Where could a sideways shift help you navigate a rigid system or stressful moment?
6. How does your wellness routine influence your creativity?

Bridge to Chapter 18

Criticism tests your voice, but compassion through self-care strengthens it. Visibility starts with small actions, but it grows when people can see who you are. Once they look you up, your profile should make it easy to understand your work, your message, and how to connect with you. Before we go any further, let's make sure your foundation is strong. In the next chapter, we'll walk through what you need for a complete profile and how to bring those pieces together with clarity.

18

BUILDING A COMPLETE PROFILE: YOUR DIGITAL HANDSHAKE

Why Your Profile Matters

A thoughtful profile does quiet work for you. It can bring in 30 percent more weekly views and open doors long before you ever speak. People take in more than we realize in just a few seconds. Your presence often says more than the post itself.

Core Elements of a Strong Profile

1. Profile Photo

Choose a recent, clear headshot with good lighting and a simple background. Photos that show your real smile or eyes tend to reach more people. Think of it as the moment someone feels welcomed in.

2. Banner Image

This is the space that tells your story at a glance. It can reflect your work, your mission, or simply your personality. A strong banner makes a profile feel memorable.

3. Headline

This is the second most searched part of your profile after your name. Instead of a job title, think about what you help others do. A simple value-focused line, such as "Helping educators and leaders build visibility with purpose," helps people understand you at a glance.

4. About Section

This is your why. Write it the way you would speak it. Keep it human and mission-centered, free of jargon. Most readers want to know three things:

- what you do and why it matters
- who you help and how
- how to connect with you

5. Experience

Share your impact, not just duties. Use language that reflects what you created, led, or changed. Let your work speak through the results and moments you are proud of.

6. Skills and Endorsements

Five to ten relevant skills help LinkedIn understand your strengths and show your profile to the right people. Update them as you grow.

7. Creator Mode (Optional)

If you enjoy sharing insights or teaching through your posts, Creator Mode can help your work reach more people. It adds a "Follow" button and a few extra features that highlight your content.

A Note About Your Photo and Banner

Make the most of your profile's visual space. Canva makes it simple to design a banner that reflects what you do. If you do not yet have a brand color palette, think about the feeling you want people to associate with your work, whether it is calm, creative, professional, or bold.

Once I served on a hiring committee for a mid-year school opening. One applicant had excellent grades, glowing recommendations, and clear confidence, yet she was not chosen. Someone on the panel said, "Something about her was off." Nothing was off except her outfit. She happened to be wearing the colors of our rival school. That moment stayed with me. I often remind interns to be mindful of the visual signals they send, from color choices to profile images. Every detail communicates something before you speak.

If you list hobbies, choose ones that matter to the audience you hope to reach. A school district might connect more with "avid reader" or "volunteer soccer coach" than "loves hanging out at the mall." And please use a recent photo. There is a running joke among event planners about people sending headshots and then showing up twenty years later looking nothing like the image.

I once experienced this when hiring a director for my solo performance. After interviewing seventeen candidates, I short-listed my favorites, only to realize I could not match anyone's current look to their submitted photos.

If you are job hunting or looking for clients, an up-to-date photo helps people remember who they met and builds trust. A great photo quietly says, "This is me now, confident, approachable, and real."

Digital Profile Checklist: Your Complete and Compelling Handshake

- Use a clear, recent headshot with good lighting and a simple background.
- Add a banner image that reflects your mission or personality.
- Write a headline that highlights the value you bring, not just your title.
- Craft an About section that feels conversational and purpose driven.
- Share accomplishments and impact in your Experience section.
- Select five to ten relevant skills, gather endorsements, and update them as you grow.
- View your profile on a mobile device to be sure it displays well.
- Refresh your headline and About section regularly. Every ninety days works well.
- Keep a small folder of inspirational posts or profiles you admire.
- Ask a trusted colleague or mentor to look over your profile and offer feedback.

Banner Ideas by Profession. Just ideas...

If you create products, let people see you at work, whether you are assembling, sketching, or photographing the final piece. If you lead or coach, show moments of you with your team, in conversation, or brainstorming at a whiteboard. If you work with clients, a photo of you listening or collaborating communicates professionalism and warmth. If you design or innovate, show your workspace, your laptop, your sketches, or your prototypes so people can see creativity in motion. If you are a consultant or strategist, a clean background with data charts or subtle branding elements works well.

Your banner should simply show you doing what you do best, whether that is creating, leading, collaborating, or building. It tells your story before a single word is read.

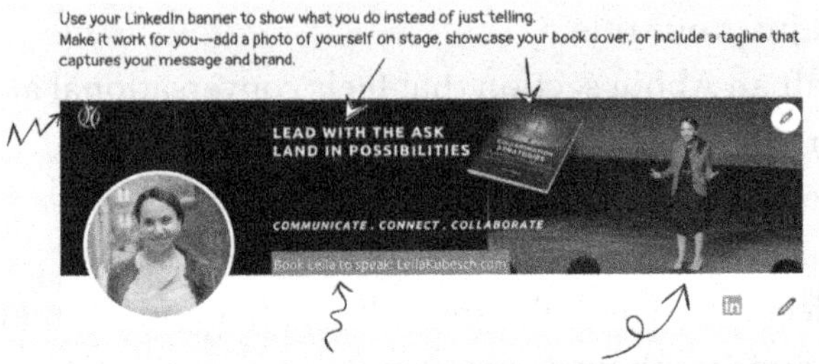

Tips for a Strong Profile

- Take a quick look at your profile on your phone. Most people meet you there first.
- Choose a banner that reflects your mission or the spirit of your work.
- Keep a small folder of posts or profiles that inspire you.
- Refresh your headline and About section every so often so they match who you are now.

Chapter Summary

- A strong profile feels like a warm digital handshake.
- People respond to clarity, authenticity, and a complete picture of who you are.
- Photos and headlines carry more weight than we realize.
- Results and stories draw people in far more than a list of duties.

- Creator Mode is helpful if you enjoy sharing ideas and want your work to reach more people.

Reflection & Application

1.What impression does your profile give to a first-time visitor?

2.Which sections feel incomplete or outdated?

3.What story or skill could you add today to reflect who you are now?

4.What is one small change you could make to increase authenticity?

Bridge to Chapter 19

Your profile gets people in the door, but your voice is what stays with them. Now comes the part most people avoid and where your visibility starts to accelerate. A camera, good lighting, one take. That is all it takes to create a short that travels farther than you ever will. Some of my simplest videos made the biggest impact. If you are ready for that kind of momentum, turn the page. The next chapter shows you how to record yourself in a way that feels natural and gets noticed.

19

RECORD YOURSELF WITHOUT CRINGING

After my ninth retake, I wasn't sure if I was finally pleased with the result or just tired of seeing myself on screen. Probably the first. Recording helped me become more aware of my mannerisms and work on eliminating them. I used to sway back and forth while recording because, in my head, I was alternating between languages, and somehow my body followed the rhythm. Somewhere in that final round, I stopped overthinking, dropped the head tilts, and let the mannerisms fall away. That's when I discovered that watching yourself enough becomes self-discovery. Each take is a mirror, reflecting not your flaws but your progress.

You don't need to spend a lot of money or buy fancy equipment to start. Many of the most viewed videos online are far from perfect. They aren't beautifully lit or flawlessly edited, but they capture something real, and real connects.

I've watched many successful people build influence through simple, unpolished videos filmed in basements or kitchens while wearing a plain T-shirt with their logo. They didn't try to impress; they just showed up to share value. Meanwhile, I used to spend hours thinking, "I can't record today! My hair isn't done, my nails aren't polished, I don't know what to wear." I'd debate between a blazer and a hoodie and continue avoiding the camera. Eventually, I learned that perfection only delays purpose. What matters most is your message.

How to Prepare Your Space

The space behind you matters more than what's in front of you. No one sees the pile of papers near your keyboard, but they'll notice a messy background. Keep what's behind you calm, simple, and distraction-free. Avoid open doors, background movement, and clutter. You don't need a designer setup. A plain wall, bookshelf, or curtain works just fine.

Skip virtual backgrounds. They often glitch, blur your outline, or make your arm or head disappear when you move.. Keep it real and neutral to keep the focus on you. Lighting is your best friend. Face a window if possible. Natural light is flattering and free. If that's not an option, use a basic ring light. Make sure your face is well-lit and your clothing contrasts with your background so you don't blend in.

Create a List of Topics

Before you press record, know what you'll say. Keep a running list of short, meaningful topics your audience will care about—simple questions, lessons learned, or quick insights. Each one can become a 60-second video. You don't need a script. Just jot down three things: a hook, your story, and the takeaway. That's all you need to sound focused and natural. If it still feels difficult, try using Otter.ai. It records your voice and gives you the exact words you said. You can use it while walking, when ideas come to mind, or while doing other tasks. This way, you can keep your thoughts safe. I turn those notes into bullet points or short scripts. My favorite teleprompter app is SpeakFlow because it highlights what to say next.

How to Speak Naturally on Camera

Posture changes everything. Sit or stand tall so your voice projects confidence. If you slump, your breath shortens and your energy drops. Stretch your neck and shoulders. Have a sip of warm tea, not coffee or ice water to soothe your tone. Nerves are normal.

If your voice trembles, smile as you begin. It instantly softens your tone and boosts confidence. Imagine you're talking to one person who believes in you, not a faceless crowd. If you aim to be perfect, nothing will get done. I met a professional news reporter who wanted to become a speaker. She always said it wasn't the right time, that she didn't have space at home, or that she needed to look perfect first. In the end, she never gave herself a chance to be visible.

If You Don't Have a Teleprompter

You don't need a teleprompter to sound polished. If you forget your lines, type them in a large font and center them on your screen. Leave wide margins so your eyes don't dart too far. Position your text close to the camera, scroll slowly, and keep your eyes near the lens. That maintains a connection while letting you glance naturally at your notes. If you're using cue cards or outlines, tape them beside your camera and practice reading aloud until your voice flows easily.

Stay Ready

"Don't get ready. Stay ready." —Craig Valentine, 1999 World Champion of Public Speaking

This quote stays taped near my desk. It reminds me that visibility is a mindset. Prepare the day before. Gather your notes. If you don't have a dedicated space for recording, tell your family in advance. Keep a simple "Recording" sign on your door so no one barges in mid-sentence. When your space is ready, your confidence follows.

Tips & Resources to Show Up Well on Camera

You don't need to be an influencer to belong on camera. You just need to show up as yourself. LinkedIn and nearly every platform now favor video content. You don't need a fancy studio or confidence you don't yet have. You only need intention, light, and a plan.

1. Let the Light Love You

- Natural light is still the best filter.
- Face a window if you can; never sit with it behind you.
- At night, use a simple front light like NexiGo or Engitube. • Avoid mixing warm and cool bulbs.

Tip: If you can clearly see your palm lines when you hold up your hand, the light is good.

2. Camera Height and Angle

- Your camera should meet your eyes, not your chin.
- Use a tripod, stack of books, or box to reach the right height.
- Look into the lens, not your reflection.
- Tape a small sticky note near the lens with a grounding word.

3. The Sound of Credibility

- People will forgive a blurry video before they forgive bad sound.
- Use a small microphone if possible. The RØDE Wireless GO II is excellent.

- If you're on a budget, use wired earbuds.
- Record in a quiet space and don't stress over perfection.

4. Body Language That Speaks Calm

- Sit up straight with your shoulders back.
- Gesture naturally.
- Speak at a calm pace with steady breath.
- Smile slightly before speaking to soften your tone.

5. What to Say and How Plan your first line—that's all. The rest will flow. A great first line is your hook. For example, "Here's something I wish I knew when I started." Keep videos under two minutes unless you're teaching something detailed. End with an invitation: "What's your experience with this?" or "Would this help your team?"

6. Editing Without the Headache • Skip complicated software. • Try Descript—it lets you edit by editing text and adds captions automatically. • Always include captions since many viewers watch on mute.

7. The Mindset Shift Everyone feels awkward at first. Start anyway. Film five clips you never post. Practice comfort before content. The best time to learn is now. You can't edit the draft you never create.

Editing & Repurposing with Ease: Mini-Guide

You don't need to post every day to stay visible. You need to post with purpose, then repurpose what works. Most people record once and move on. The pros make one message work twelve ways.

1. Record Once, Use Often

- Turn a video into a post, a quote graphic, a newsletter, or a blog.
- Add clips to future talks or trainings. If you record weekly, you'll have a year's worth of content even posting twice a month.

2. **Start with What's Already Working** Review past posts that got comments or saves. Repurpose those ideas instead of starting over. Consistency builds recognition.

3. **Batch Your Creativity** Record three to five videos in one sitting. Change outfits or accessories for variety. Pretend you're talking to a favorite client or friend to shift from "presentation" to "conversation."

4. **Automate** Use free tools like Buffer or Canva's Scheduler. Set one day a month to upload and schedule. Automation keeps you visible without daily effort.

5. **Let Your Imperfections Work for You** The videos that go viral aren't the most polished—they're the most real. If your light flickers or your cat walks across the screen, keep going. That's the charm people remember.

Ask, Don't Tell End your posts with real questions. Instead of saying "Leadership is about service," ask "Who's one leader you've met who led with service?" When you invite others to share, your post becomes a conversation, and engagement grows naturally.

Chapter Summary

- Light yourself from the front.
- Keep your camera at eye level.
- Ensure sound is clear.
- Speak from the heart, not a script.
- Batch and automate your process.

- Remember: authenticity beats perfection.

Questions Worth Asking • What's one post or story I could turn into three pieces of content this week? • Am I editing to impress or to express? • Could I teach this same message through a video, post, and quote? • Would I watch this if someone else posted it? • Am I showing up as who I am—or who I think is expected?

Reflection Poem — "Press Record Anyway"

Your hair's not right, your voice feels small,
you trip on words, forget it all.

You sigh, restart, and lose your way—
then think, I'll try another day.

But someone waits to hear your view,
your story might be what pulls them through.

Don't wait for perfect, stage, or say—
just breathe it out and press record today.

Each take you make, each try you do,
will shape the strength that's growing in you.

No need for polish, praise, or fame—
just heart, just courage, just your name.

Leila Kubesch

Reflection & Application

1. What small improvement can you make to your setup this week?

2. What story deserves to be shared next?

3. How can you make your space feel like a creative zone, not a chore?

4. Who needs to hear your voice and not just read your words?

Bridge to chapter 20

As you grow your presence online, not every click or connection will have good intentions. The more visible you become, the more careful you need to be. The next chapter is about guarding your glow and protecting your digital boundaries so opportunity doesn't become vulnerability.

20

GUARD YOUR GLOW BY PROTECTING YOUR DIGITAL BOUNDARIES

I received a direct message on LinkedIn that looked legitimate. The profile seemed real, the tone was professional, and the sender invited me to check out a new website that listed paid speaking opportunities for professionals like me. It looked promising, so I clicked the link and filled out the form. As soon as I finished, a pop-up appeared asking me to grant access to my Google account. That made me pause. Why would a site that already displayed event planners, conference names, and high speaker fees need access to my Google account?

A few minutes later, I received another direct message from the same person, this time offering to "walk me through the site" by having remote access to my computer. Remote access? Why not a Zoom call or a short tutorial video? The site itself was simple; there was no need for a walkthrough or tour.

That's when it clicked. This wasn't an opportunity, it was a setup. I logged out immediately, made sure any Google permissions I had ever granted were revoked, and changed my password.

Online safety is about boundaries that protect, not limit, opportunities.

When the Promise Turns into a Trap

What hurts most in these moments isn't just the violation of trust; it's realizing how easily professional polish can be mistaken for trustworthiness. The internet can make everything look legitimate, and scammers know that.

Here's what I learned, and what I want you to remember:

1. **Slow down when it sounds urgent.** Scammers use pressure to cloud judgment, using phrases like "limited time!" and "immediate action required." Anything demanding an instant response deserves a pause. Real opportunities allow time to think.
2. **Verify before you trust.** Look up the sender's name and organization on LinkedIn or an official site. Hover over links before clicking to see where they really lead. When in doubt, reply separately (never in the same thread) and ask for clarification.
3. **Guard your personal information.** Never send ID, payment details, or unpublished material before verifying the contact. I now watermark early drafts, use restricted file links, and only share excerpts when a contract is signed.
4. **Use a "Pause Folder."** When something excites you, drop it in a folder labeled *Wait 24 Hours.* That pause between emotion and action can save you from regret.
5. **Protect your emotional bandwidth.** If a mistake is made, don't let shame become another thief. We can't always control deception, but we can control how we grow from it.

When Opportunity Masks Risk

Not every door that opens deserves to be walked through. Sometimes the best yes begins with a confident no. Before granting access or downloading any tool, pause and ask:

- Does this need full access to my data, or just basic info?
- Is this company verified by professionals I trust?
- If my data were misused, how easily could I recover?

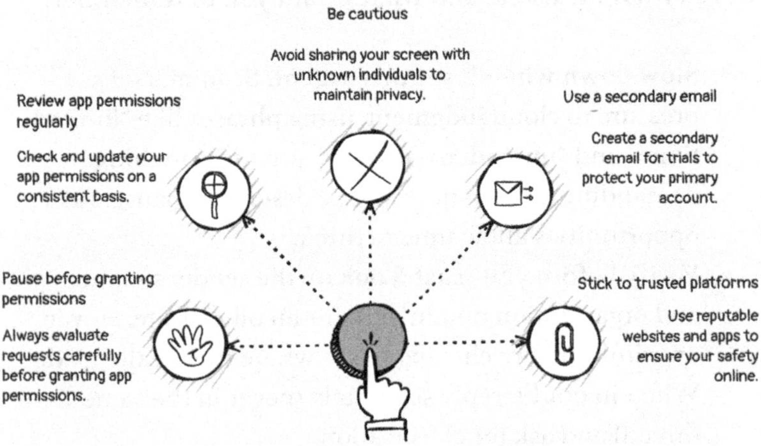

Safety Checklist

- Pause before granting permission.
- Stick to trusted platforms.
- Review app and site permissions regularly.
- Use a secondary email for trials or testing.
- Never share your screen with strangers.
- Question convenience.
- Share your stories because they might protect someone else.

When you share your screen, you're opening a window into your digital world—and that can be risky. The other person might see things you didn't plan to share, like passwords, private messages, or files with personal or work details. They could even record what's on your screen and keep it. Sometimes, people use screen sharing to trick others into clicking links or opening files that can harm your computer.

Even if you trust them, hidden software or malware could still expose your data. Before sharing, close extra tabs, turn off notifications, and share only the window you really need.

Safe Files: Before You Open Anything • Acceptable file types: .jpg, .png, .gif, .tif • Avoid opening: .exe, .scr — these install software, not images. • Large or unexpected files? ⚐ Stop and verify first.

A few seconds of caution can save hours of damage. Check suspicious files at **VirusTotal.com.**

Resources to Protect Your Digital Presence

- For secure file sharing, set Google Drive "view only" or use Dropbox watermarked links.
- Report scams to **reportphishing@apwg.org** or **FTC.gov/scams.**
- Check Google account permissions using **myaccount.google.com/permissions.**

Chapter Summary

- Visibility attracts both risk and reward.
- Professional polish isn't proof of trustworthiness—always verify.
- Boundaries sustain opportunity.
- Urgency and convenience are red flags.

- Every cautionary story protects someone else's glow.

Reflection & Application

1. Which of your online habits leaves you most exposed or drained?

2. When did you last pause before clicking send?

3. If your attention was your most valuable currency, how would you spend it differently when online?

Bridge to Chapter 20

Sometimes I wonder if there's any real perk to paying for a membership when we can already access most things for free.That changed the day I had a serious issue and needed to reach the top, past every gatekeeper standing in the way. Suddenly, having direct access mattered.That experience changed how I think about value, access, and what it means to have a door you can walk through when you need it most.

21

DO YOU NEED LINKEDIN PREMIUM TO GROW?

Should you become a Premium member to grow your following on LinkedIn? My answer is no. My 23,000+ followers came long before I ever paid for LinkedIn Premium. You don't need it to build visibility or engagement. You only need consistency. Still, I do have Premium now and here's why.

The Zumba Lesson

A few years ago, I moved from one state to another. My husband made friends easily while I was starting from scratch in new community with no familiar faces. One day, I walked into the local YMCA and asked at the front desk, "What exactly is Zumba?" She didn't answer my question. Instead, she smiled and whispered, "Honey, make sure you come five minutes early. The class fills up fast." Eager, I showed up ten minutes early to be at the end of the class. Within minutes, the studio was packed shoulder to shoulder, wall to wall.

The music began and arms were flying, hips turning. I tried to follow the person in front of me because being short, I couldn't even see the instructor. I ended up staying a few beats behind. Eventually, I stopped paying attention and started doing my own thing. Just as I started to have fun, the instructor shouted, "Okay, people in the back, you're now the front! Face the back wall, everyone!"

My heart sank. I wasn't ready to be seen. I didn't know the steps, but I couldn't leave because my bag with my phone and keys was too far. I stayed and I kept moving. How do they know how to dance like that? I didn't have that Latin rhythm. I grew up in North Africa, and all I knew was the beat of the drum that made me shimmy and sway my hips. Still, I didn't give up. I found out there was a way to become certified as an instructor and thought, if I can teach it, then I can do it just as well as anyone on that dance floor. I found a class and signed up.

A few months later, I was back at the same gym, in that very studio, this time as the Zumba instructor!

When Membership Turns Messy

To stay certified as an instructor, I needed to join the Zumba Instructor Network (ZIN). It came with a monthly fee and offered new choreography, music, and teaching ideas monthly. It was wonderful, until I tried to cancel. Every call turned into a marathon of transfers and persuasion. It was a nightmare. Years later, when I decided to rejoin, I paid with a Visa gift card just in case. Sure enough, the cancellation process was just as exhausting. At one point, they even warned me they would work to ruin my credit.

That moment shifted something in me. I was very upset, but instead of arguing, I paid for the months I didn't want and then took action. I reached out directly to all the Zumba leaders on LinkedIn, calmly explained my experience, and within twenty minutes, I received a phone call and a full refund. Not everyone at the top is aware of what happens below them.

That call taught me a lifelong truth: asking clearly, calmly, and directly can solve more than confrontation ever will.

The Real Power of Premium

That Zumba experience was my warm-up for understanding LinkedIn Premium. It's not about access to fame, it's about access to people.

LinkedIn Premium doesn't automatically bring followers. What it does provide is direct outreach, visibility analytics, and access to hundreds of professional online trainings, from communication and leadership to social media, storytelling, and AI. It's like a professional gym for your mind. The membership alone won't create change, but consistently using its resources can transform how you work and grow. The more you apply what you learn, the more you'll see progress, in your business and in yourself.

When I see an event or organization that aligns with my message, I don't wait for a call for speakers. I use Premium to contact decision-makers directly, event organizers, communications directors, HR leads.

My message is a simple "Hi [Name], I noticed you're involved with [event]. I'd love to connect you with a resource and I'm also curious who I can reach out to about your keynote lineup." That approach has led to speaking invitations in the U.S. and abroad.

How to Use It Wisely

Start small. Use the free trial first, then choose the lowest-tier plan to see if it helps you.

Research strategically. Use Premium to identify event planners, universities, and companies aligned with your work.

Use LinkedIn Learning. There's a library of short, high-quality video trainings on every topic imaginable, including leadership, productivity, storytelling, and communication.

Message intentionally. Write short, direct notes that sound human.

Set a reminder to cancel or renew. Never let billing cycles surprise you.

Lessons Learned

When you join any membership, online or offline, lead with curiosity, not cynicism. Ask questions, take notes, and keep records. If something goes wrong, reach out to the right person rather than react with frustration. Most organizations want to make things right, they just need to hear from someone calm, clear, and kind.

Why I Stayed

Eventually, I decided to keep my Premium account. It helps me reach people I wouldn't otherwise meet, grow my visibility with purpose, and continue learning through its training library.

Chapter Summary

- You don't need Premium to grow, you need purpose and persistence.
- Access without clarity leads to waste of money. Access with focus builds opportunity.
- The real power of Premium lies in learning and outreach, not visibility metrics.
- Sometimes the best opportunities come from the messages you send, not the ones you wait to receive.
- Confidence is built by showing up before you feel ready.

Reflection & Application

1. What membership or tool are you using out of habit, and does it still serve your goals?

2. How could curiosity replace hesitation in your next professional step?

3. What skill could you improve this month through a short online training?

4. Who could you reach out to directly, instead of waiting to be found?

Bridge to Chapter 22

You don't need hacks or shortcuts. You need systems that multiply your time and protect your energy. The next chapter walks you through tools that keep your visibility growing even when you step away from the screen.

22

THE POD: PAID PRAISE IS PROHIBITED

Not long after I started posting regularly on LinkedIn, a message landed in my inbox that read almost too well to ignore. “We can help you grow faster. Guaranteed likes, comments, and visibility. Real people, real engagement!” The offer? A membership-based pod. At first glance, it looked like a supportive community of professionals boosting one another’s posts. But then came the fine print, a monthly fee.

That’s when I learned that pods really are groups of people who agree to comment and like each other’s content for a price. It’s engagement on demand. Except it isn’t real. A paid pod is an echo chamber of fake applause, a place where authenticity goes to die. And beyond the ethics, it’s strictly against LinkedIn’s rules. Accounts that engage in this kind of paid praise can, and often do, get deactivated.

Stay away. No shortcut is worth losing your account.

The Illusion of Paid Engagement

Buying likes doesn't foster genuine connections.

Paid Likes Don't Lead to Real Leads

Buying engagement is like planting plastic flowers.
They look bright for a while, but they don't grow roots.
The goal of visibility isn't applause. It's awareness.
You want the right people to find you — not just anyone.
When you earn engagement, you build reputation.
When you buy it, you build noise.

Why People Fall for It

Pods appeal to our human need for validation. If you post and no one reacts, the silence stings. Then when someone promises a quick fix, a circle of guaranteed engagement, it might seem like the answer you were hoping for. However, the truth is that fake engagement teaches the wrong audience.

Sure, you'll get likes, but you won't get a connection. People can spot inauthentic comments instantly. Comments like "so true!", "amazing insight!" or "love this!" are praise without presence and it hurts your credibility. If you are curious, feel free to try. I don't give advice.

What Actually Works

Real growth takes relationships. When you show up consistently, share meaningful ideas, and engage with others from a place of curiosity, you'll eventually build your own tribe.

Every time I speak at a conference, several attendees come up to connect afterward. They comment, share my posts, and sometimes that connection fades over time, while other times it lasts for years. That's the kind of engagement that sticks because it's built on real connection. If you nurture that community, it will grow naturally. Sometimes it slows down when you're less active, but it never disappears because it's built on trust.

What to Do Instead

Comment with intention. Engage with others before expecting them to engage with you.

Write something worth responding to. Ask a genuine question or share a story others can add to.

Build your circle, not a paid pod. Two or three thoughtful voices are better than fifty empty comments.

Track authentic growth. Notice who keeps showing up, those are your real people.

Remember that algorithms reward consistency, but humans reward sincerity. It also changes frequently.

Why Some People Can't Comment on Your LinkedIn Posts Anymore

In November 2025, I tried to comment on a friend's post like I usually do, but this time it didn't work. Every time I tried, a message appeared saying, *"This post cannot be displayed. The author has restricted who can view this post."*

I asked LinkedIn's Help Desk what happened. They explained that LinkedIn no longer has one main setting that lets everyone comment on your posts. Now, you have to choose who can comment each time you post something. This change gives users more control over privacy. It also means that if someone isn't your connection, they can't comment unless you change the setting for that specific post.

Chapter Summary

- Paid pods are fake communities that can cost you your credibility and your account.
- Authentic engagement builds visibility that lasts.
- True influence grows through curiosity, consistency, and care.
- Your real team finds you when you show up as yourself, not as your strategy

What Not to Do on Linkedin

Don't post to post, just take your time,
Silence can speak — it isn't a crime.

Don't chase a trend you don't believe,
Be real, be you, and don't deceive.

Skip "honored, thrilled," that tired song,
Say what happened, short and strong.

Don't write like PR on parade,
Speak like a friend whose trust you've made.

Don't ghost your post once it's begun,
The comments are where hearts are won.

Don't frame perfection in every shot,
A real face shines — filters do not.

Don't bleed online before you heal,
Share the wisdom, not the ordeal.

Don't pitch in DMs to make a sale,
Connection first — that never fails.

Don't chase the clicks, the reach, the chart,
Write from your gut, not from a part.

Don't tag a crowd to chase a view,
Honor the ones who walk with you.

Don't think the quiet ones don't care,
They're watching — and they'll soon be there.

So post with grace, and keep it kind,
Your story's gold — when heart aligns with mind.

Leila Kubesch

Reflection & Application

1. Would I still post this if no one liked it?

2. Who genuinely engages with my work and how can I nurture that?

3. How can I make my presence online reflect who I am offline?

4. What would my digital footprint say if someone scrolled through it a year from now?

Bridge to Chapter 23

Visibility grows fastest when it's authentic. The next chapter explores what not to do, including how paid praise and engagement pods can quietly undo the credibility you've worked so hard to build.You don't need hacks or shortcuts. You need systems that multiply your time and protect your energy. The next chapter walks you through tools that keep your visibility growing even when you step away from the screen.

23

TOOLS THAT PROTECT YOUR ENERGY

I used to believe that increasing your productivity meant doing more. Now I know it means protecting what matters most, your time. Every idea, post, or project depends on how well you manage your attention. Using right tools doesn't just save time, it saves your energy. They can free your mind to focus on what truly counts, creating, connecting, and resting.

Below are the tools I use and trust. They've been tested, broken, fixed, and tested again. Think of them as quiet partners that help keep you visible without burning you out.

1. Canva: Designing made Simple

When someone tells me they are not creative, I point them to Canva. It is the easiest way to make your brand look polished, even if your design experience ended with PowerPoint.

What I use it for:

- Banners, flyers, and speaker slides
- Newsletter headers and social posts
- Video and promo graphics

Create one simple template you love, duplicate it, and adjust the colors as you go. Consistency builds trust quietly and fast. If you work with interns or assistants, share your Canva folder so everyone stays aligned.

2. **Descript:** Audio and Video Made Human

I used to dread video editing until I discovered Descript. It lets you edit video by editing text, which feels natural and intuitive. Delete a sentence in the transcript and the video follows.

Great for:

- Turning keynote clips into short social videos
- Repurposing trainings into smaller lessons
- Podcast intros and teasers

You can record inside Descript or upload a clip from your phone. Use it to capture quick ideas that may become your next post or pitch.

3. **QuillBot:** Polish Without Losing Your Voice

Sometimes you are too close to your writing to see it clearly. QuillBot helps simplify without stripping your tone. You can choose the style that feels right, from formal to conversational.

Let AI support you, not replace you. Read everything out loud before sharing. Your voice is your fingerprint, so keep it intact.

4. **WiseStamp:** Quiet Branding in Every Inbox

Refresh your signature every so often so it reflects your newest offer, article, or keynote. Visibility grows through small touches that gently repeat your message.

5. **Otter.Ai:** Capture Your Thoughts in Real Time

Otter is a voice recording and transcription tool that turns spoken words into clear, searchable text. It is helpful for capturing ideas, meetings, interviews, and moments of inspiration. You can highlight, edit, and share notes easily.

Record from your phone or computer. It keeps your ideas close, organized, and easy to return to when you are ready to shape them.

6. GoHighLevel: The System That Simplified Everything

This platform changed how I run my business. Instead of juggling separate tools for emails, landing pages, scheduling, forms, and communication, everything now lives in one place. There is a learning curve, but once you settle into it, you will wonder how you ever worked without it.

At the time of this writing, it is about ninety seven dollars a month and replaces many subscriptions that used to scatter my attention across multiple platforms.

Scan the QR code or use the link above.

Start small. Even automating one repetitive task makes a meaningful difference.

7. Hoopla: Read Without Excuses

Your library card gives you access to free ebooks and audiobooks. If your library uses Hoopla, you can borrow instantly with no waiting lists. If they use Libby or another partner instead, the experience is just as easy.

Before a flight or walk, download a few audiobooks. Listening is one of the most affordable ways to fill your mind with better ideas for posts, talks, and inspiration.

Chapter Summary

- Digital tools do not replace creativity. They free the time and effort you lose to repetitive tasks, leaving you available for the work only you can do.
- Tools save time, but boundaries save sanity.
- You may not need more hours in your day. You may need fewer distractions.
- Technology works best when it helps you stay human.

Reflection & Application

1. Which tool could free up the most mental space for you, not just minutes?
2. What repetitive task could you automate this month?
3. How would your work change if your systems worked as quietly and efficiently as you do?

AFTERWORD

This book began in the classroom, surrounded by students who reminded me that courage often starts quietly. Their willingness to try new things, even when they were uncertain of their abilities, sparked my own journey to learn, ask, and share in new ways.

To my fellow educators who have taught me the art of patience, humor, and heart, I thank you for showing up when the world asked more of you. You remind me daily that teaching is not just about lessons but lasting impact.

To the colleagues, mentors, and speaking peers who encouraged me to keep writing when it felt easier to stay invisible, your belief made this possible. A special thank you to the National Speakers Association community for the camaraderie, laughter, and lessons that continue to expand what is possible.

To my family, thank you for giving me the space to dream, to fail, and to begin again.

And to you, the reader, thank you for taking the time to read and reflect. I'd love to stay connected. Let's keep the conversation going.

You're Everywhere!

You showed up scared but spoke out loud,
Now look at you—you're wowing the crowd!
On LinkedIn, Insta, TikTok too,
The world's gone brighter—all from you.

Your Wi-Fi's strong, your light's just right,
You post with courage, laugh at night.
Onstage, online, you found your flair—
Face it, friend… you're *everywhere!*

So keep on shining, flaws and all,
Answer the dream when you hear it call.
No need for filters, likes, or share—
You've claimed your voice—you're already there.

Leila Kubesch

ABOUT THE AUTHOR

About the Author (as written by the publisher)

Leila Kubesch is an educator, storyteller, and international keynote speaker known for transforming everyday challenges into opportunities for connection. Named the 2020 Ohio Teacher of the Year and inducted into the National Teachers Hall of Fame, she blends humor, heart, and practical insight to inspire action. Her work has been featured at TEDx, The Moth, and in classrooms around the world where she helps educators, leaders, and change-makers embrace visibility without losing authenticity. Through her 3 Cs movement: Communicate, Connect, and Collaborate, Leila equips others to turn small sparks of courage into lasting impact. She is also the founder of Parents2Partners.org, a nonprofit organization that empowers families and educators to work together for student success. When she's not speaking or writing, you'll find her behind the camera capturing the quiet joy of people learning and leading together.

To connect or learn more, visit LeilaKubesch.com and find her on LinkedIn.

About the Author (Preferred bio)

About Leila

Award-winning teacher, wife, lives with her dog and passionate about making a difference!

Leila keeps you on track, makes you laugh, and somehow turns every challenge into fun. She's resourceful, real, and her classes feel like a mix of learning and stand-up comedy — you leave smarter and smiling.

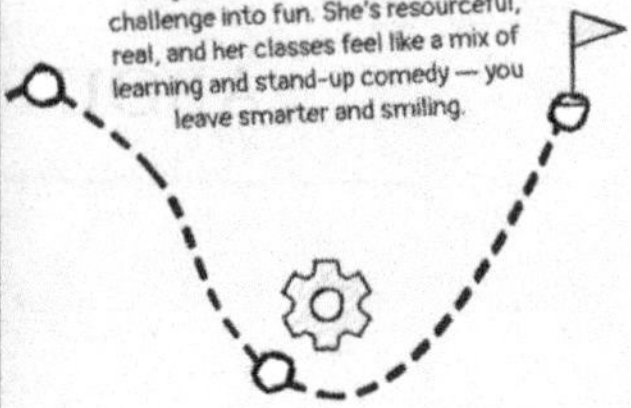

Made in the USA
Monee, IL
04 November 2026

67385351R00089